Maurizio Ferraris
Webfare

Editorial

Today's rapid technological and scientific progress has unforeseeable epistemic and social side effects. An apt approach must take into account the complex dynamics of social conditions and realities associated with scientific practices of knowledge production and their implementation in technology.

The book series **Technosophy**, published at the "Center for Science and Thought" (CST) of the University of Bonn, presents interdisciplinary work from philosophy, the humanities and social sciences that contributes to wiser uses of technology, and to interpretations of cutting-edge science, both grounded in their very ontologies and epistemologies.

The series is edited by Markus Gabriel, Dennis Lehmkuhl, Aimee van Wynsberghe and Ana Ilievska. Managing editors are Christiane Schäfer and Jan Voosholz.

Maurizio Ferraris is a full professor of theoretical philosophy at the University of Turin. He is the president of Labont (Center for Ontology) and also the president of "Scienza Nuova", an institute of advanced studies aimed at planning a sustainable future. Visiting professor at Harvard, Oxford, Munich, and Paris, newspaper columnist, author of successful television programmes and over seventy books, he has determined a new course of thought and studies in at least six areas: history of hermeneutics, aesthetics as theory of perception, social ontology, metaphysics, technological anthropology, and philosophy of economics.

Maurizio Ferraris

Webfare

A Manifesto for Digital Well-Being

[transcript]

"Webfare: A Manifesto for Digital Well-Being" was created at the University of Bonn. Its publication was made possible by the support of the Open Access publication fund of the University of Bonn and of the Stiftung Mercator.

Bibliographic information published by the Deutsche Nationalbibliothek
The Deutsche Nationalbibliothek lists this publication in the Deutsche Nationalbibliografie

First published in 2024 by transcript Verlag, Bielefeld
© Maurizio Ferraris

Cover layout: Maria Arndt, Bielefeld
Cover illustration: Montage by Joline Kretschmer, "John Maynard Keynes,
    Baron Keynes" by Gwen Raverat © National Portrait Gallery, London
translated by Dr. Ana Ilievska, Bonn
Printed by: Majuskel Medienproduktion GmbH, Wetzlar
https://doi.org/10.14361/9783839471760
Print-ISBN: 978-3-8376-7176-6
PDF-ISBN: 978-3-8394-7176-0
EPUB-ISBN: 978-3-7328-7176-6
ISSN of series: 2943-2987

Contents

Growth or Degrowth? Maurizio Ferraris's Economy of Digital Waste Recycling

Preface by Ana Ilievska (Bonn)

Can we produce value simply by virtue of being human? Should and can we reconcile ourselves to being consumers rather than producers? Should we earn according to our merit or our needs? Can we reconsider 'growth' and 'capitalization' rather than promote a return to some primitivist utopia? If there can be recycling bins for banana peels, Amazon boxes, and plastic bottles, why cannot there be digital bins that would recycle and thus render valuable the 'data waste' that we create during our most banal activities? Maurizio Ferraris's *Webfare* raises many questions like these that some might perceive as provocative or naïve, others as realistic. *In primis*, however, this short book asks us to reconsider the essence—if there is one—of what it means to be human in the twenty-first century. Going against conceptions of the human as *homo laborans* or *homo faber*—the working animal or the animal that creates—Ferraris proposes a view of humans as needy consumers. This description is, of course, not very flattering. But it is based on a simple anthropological fact that is not to be confused with reckless consumerism in the capitalist sense: in the face of nature, the human animal is intrinsically helpless (what Ferraris calls our 'first' nature) and in need of technology in order to survive (our 'second' nature). We still our intrinsic neediness through accumulation or storing for future use (also known as capitalization), and by constant consumption: "We produce for future consumption, and the only animals truly capable of consumption are human animals" (16). This essence of ours as the needy animal goes hand in hand with technology, viz., there is no such thing as a human before technology:

"From the outset, human nature has been a second nature—the result of the interplay between organisms and mechanisms, soul and automaton" (61). Humans are what they are *because* of technology, whether by technology we mean language, a stick, or ChatGPT: "to become human," Ferraris writes, "means to develop increasingly sophisticated technologies" (ibidem) within the "techno-anthropological circle" (60ff). As infinite beings, machines have no internal purpose, no *needs*, but we do. In this sense, both our and the existence of machines is dependent on the feedback we give one another. Being more than just animals and far less than gods, we create machines in order to come to terms with our liminal existence. Indeed, technology would have no place among angels. The existence of technology presupposes imperfection.

Now such a conception of the human machine relationship is not unproblematic for it implies a potentially destructive co-dependency and an ever-escalating disregard for environmental and political issues in the race to secure resources. I will focus on one of its aspects in this brief introduction: the need for **growth.** Indeed, Ferraris's view of the techno-anthropological circle presupposes something like infinite or at least indefinite growth and sees continuous technological progress as being intrinsic to human civilization. He writes, "[a]dressing the pressing social and environmental issues at hand does not call for less progress, globalization, or capital, but rather demands the opposite: greater progress, precisely because it would be pursued with awareness" (91). Webfare, indeed, "is not about depressing development but harnessing its potential for the collective improvement of humanity, leading to what is effectively a happy growth" (91–2). Such a view promotes an optimistic or at least positive outlook on technological innovation against other contemporary thinkers who see human privacy, labor, and freedom imperilled in what seems to be yet another, subtler but not less harmful mutation of capitalism: surveillance capitalism and the environmental crisis and bullshit jobs that it has begotten.[1] But

---

1   See Shoshana Zuboff, *The Age of Surveillance Capitalism: The Fight for a Human Future at the New Frontier of Power* (New York: PublicAffairs, 2019); David Graeber, *Bullshit Jobs* (New York: Simon & Schuster, 2018); Kate Crawford, *Atlas of AI:*

what if growth could be re-evaluated and pursued equitably and "with awareness"? What if the traces that we leave everywhere on the Web can be accumulated and interpreted in such a way as to transform them into value which can, in turn, be redistributed to those in need? This, in a nutshell, is the core tenet of *Webfare*.

To properly understand and contextualize Ferraris's proposal, however, a comparison is in order. For growth or rather *degrowth* is a central concern of another contemporary philosopher, Kohei Saito, whose idea of "degrowth communism" has gained him millions of readers in his homeland and now all over the world.[2] Both philosophers, obvious in Saito and without explicit references in Ferraris, have Marx as their main interlocutor. While the former wants to salvage Marx by recruiting him among the ranks of environmentalists and promoters of degrowth (something unthinkable for 'traditional' Marxists), the latter stays within a traditional Marxist framework but updates such notions as 'surplus value' and 'relations of production' to fit the current form of capital for the purpose of perhaps overcoming capitalism through its own means. Furthermore, 'growth or degrowth' seems to be the central question of the recent explosion of debates on Artificial Intelligence and technological innovation in industry, politics, and the business world, and of academics alike. As a "regulation-Europe" vs. "innovation-US" narrative is taking hold of the global imaginary, Ferraris's and Saito's thought provides a philosophical justification for each side, whereby Ferraris paradoxically seems to step over to the dark side of US American capitalism and Saito over to the EU's green push for deacceleration and control. How is this to be understood?

For one, Ferraris for years now has been trying to dispel the specters of technopessimism under the banner of a techno-humanist philosophy

---

Power, Politics, and the Planetary Costs of Artificial Intelligence (New Haven: Yale UP, 2021); Naomi Klein, *This Changes Everything: Capitalism vs. the Climate* (New York: Simon & Schuster, 2014).

2   Kohei Saito, *Marx in the Anthropocene: Towards the Idea of Degrowth Communism* (Cambridge and New York: Cambridge UP, 2022).

or 'technosophy.'[3] Friend (and critic) of Derrida and, without a doubt, the most renown scholar of hermeneutics in Italy and proponent of 'New Realism,' for over a decade Ferraris has been outlining a vision of our contemporary times as a tesseract of *spheres* at the basis of which is need and which are interconnected by the traces we leave in order to fulfil those needs. Since the value generated by such a tesseract is enormous ("human heritage"), the entire edifice should be taken out of the hands of both US liberalist and Chinese communist platforms and placed in the hands of competent hermeneuticians (ideally, each one of us) who can coherently and dispassionately interpret the traces we leave on the Web:

> The true revolution brought about by the Web does not lie merely in the possibility to express our ideas, whether right or wrong, but rather in the fact that, as we express ourselves or simply engage in activities like reading, scrolling, walking, looking for restaurants or hotels, or seeking navigational guidance, these actions are meticulously recorded. Once they are recorded, they can be compared with the acts of millions of other humans, shedding light not on the ethereal skies of our thoughts and beliefs, but on the tangible soil of our actions and deeds. (50)

Such a conception of our online lives wants to dispel the myths about us living in an infosphere[4] or in the age of mass communication. Our lives on the internet as expression of our personalities and preferences or as social beings are just the tip of the iceberg according to Ferraris. The much bigger behemoth floating beneath is the massive amount of what one might call "data waste"—the traces we leave unwittingly while we are online, the time and location of our login and Google searches, the steps we take while carrying our phone in our pocket, the sleeping habits that we entrust to health apps. Ferraris calls this information the source of "syntactic data" as distinct from "semantic data" (36ff). Let me illustrate

---

3   Maurizio Ferraris and Guido Saracco, *Tecnosofia: Tecnologia e umanesimo per una scienza nuova* (Roma: Laterza, 2023).

4   Luciano Floridi, *The 4th Revolution: How the Infosphere is Reshaping Human Reality* (Oxford: Oxford UP, 2014).

this distinction: When at the end of the eighteenth century, the philosopher Immanuel Kant, also known as "the Königsberg clock," used to go on his daily walks, punctually (earning him the nickname) and consistently, he did not produce syntactic data for the mere reason that he was not carrying a cellphone in his pocket, allowing external agents to capture this data, aggregate it, and compare it to that of millions of other philosophers who like going on walks. Except for curious onlookers who recorded this habit of his in a diary or biography, there are no recordings of the exact number of steps that Kant took, the exact route that he chose, and the exact duration of his walk.

If Kant had had an iPhone, he would not have only produced what we already know as his semantic data (i.e., his philosophical writings); he would have also contributed to syntactic data, which we could access and compare, say, to that of Hegel and Fichte, and, employing our hermeneutical, interpretative skills, eventually come up with an insight into the walking behavior of seminal philosophers, perhaps publishing a study of findings and subsequently marketing a manual on how to walk like a philosopher (and perhaps become one). Such an accumulation and interpretation of data into syntactic capital not by large companies, but by capable hermeneuticians, is what Ferraris calls "human heritage"—a treasure throve of syntactic data that can be capitalized and transformed into value by "Virtue Banks" and subsequently redistributed in the form of pecuniary rewards not among philosophers, CEOs, and hermeneuticians, but among those in need. Such is the nature of what Ferraris understands as "growth" and "capitalization." He is careful to remind us of the different meanings of 'capital':

> The great misunderstanding about capital is that it exclusively refers to industrial or financial capital [...] when, in fact, "capital" is the umbrella term for any form of accumulation of skills. Therefore, civilization as a whole must be viewed as a process of capitalization. The choice we have is not between capital and the absence of capital, but between just and unjust forms of capitalization. (62)

Saito, as a young Marxist trying to reconcile the differences between reds and greens in matters concerning the environmental crisis, holds quite the opposite view. There is no such thing as 'good' or 'just' capital for capital implies growth, and growth involves constant expansion in search for new natural and human resources, usually at the cost of the Global South. The material conditions of production are continuously externalized so that various "metabolic rifts" emerge, making invisible to the northern centers the true costs of technological development:

> By constantly shifting the ecological rifts and making them invisible to the capitalist centre, the current capitalist order of society appears attractive and comfortable for a wide range of social groups in the Global North. It thus facilitates a general social consensus, while its real costs are imposed upon other social groups in the Global South. (Saito 2022, 33)

In other words, while the Kants of today are taking their walks and counting calories to stay fit, the rest of the world suffocates under the burden of global warming and labor exploitation.

Now which one of these proposals holds the promise of a better future? Is Ferraris guilty of Jameson's and Žižek's charge that it is easier to imagine the end of all life on earth than the end of capitalism? Or is he guilty of *phronesis*, the practical philosopher's attitude who seeks to make the best out of what already lies before him? What indeed, is truly *desirable*, to use the wording of the Mercator-funded project within which Ferraris's manifesto was written? Saito's proposal requires a systemic revolution, a complete overhaul of the current global economy of growth and its institutions towards "degrowth communism," a "stationary and circular economy without economic growth" as a radical alternative to "capitalism that pursues endless capital accumulation and economic growth" (Saito 207). All critique of his re-interpretation of Marx aside, is Saito's proposal *desirable* or even *viable* at all? Rather than framing Ferraris's Webfare and Saito's degrowth communism in opposition, is it perhaps more reasonable to consider them as two steps of the same process, one at its beginning and the other at its extreme end? The issue at stake here does not seem to be of economic, socio-political, or environmental nature, but is rather philosophical: the very conception of the human and its relationship to technology are at stake. Are humans capable of thinking about degrowth without associating it with such concepts as entropy or even death? Could intellectuals envision a Webfare society without associating it with capitalism and resignation? And would politicians be able to implement it without twentieth-century-déjà-vus? I believe that the problem can be solved through the simple metaphor of waste recycling for, at the end of the day, what Ferraris is proposing is precisely this: **an economy of consensual and conscientious digital waste recycling.** The only revolution that he seeks to bring about is one where society takes care of humans according to their needs and not according to their merits. Webfare is not about accepting capitalism but about accepting consumption and technology as intrinsic to being human, and to be human is to generate value.

Finally, Ferraris's proposal is more than just an essay in philosophy or political economy—it is already being implemented at the New Science Institute for Advanced Studies in Turin through collaborations with potential data intermediaries (or "Virtue Banks") such as banks, hospitals, universities, and cooperatives. The goal is to train citizens, thinkers, technologists, and simply any user with an internet access to understand data and engage critically with the web. At the end of the day, Ferraris's is a thoroughly humanistic (but not anthropocentric) project that seeks "to restore political agency, and consequently, a sense of responsibility" to humanity in view of the latest technological developments. The question whether we should pursue growth or abandon it becomes secondary. Growth is a given, and perhaps old Marx saw something essential there in human nature, and *how*—not *whether*—we pursue it, is the real challenge for our times.

Ana Ilievska
Bonn, February 2024

Prologue: Why Webfare?

Webfare, a form of digital welfare, seeks to initiate a Copernican revolution that places need instead of merit at the center of society. Need acts as an equalizer among humans, while merit serves as a differentiating factor. Furthermore, merit entails controversial choices and rests on criteria that are more often than not evanescent while there is no doubt that the thirsty are thirsty and that the hungry are hungry. Every human, just like every organism, must reckon with the empire of metabolism. Born as an organic dimension, need possesses the extraordinary capacity to evolve and become complex. It can transform into desire, will, intention, or taste thereby shaping the character of individuals and, most importantly, introducing the only possible infinity into a finite being. For it is indisputable that while even the most sublime merits are subject to limitation and finiteness, need and will are infinite and insatiable in humans, and they only end when life itself ends.

Consumption (to be differentiated from "consumerism") is the particular manner in which metabolism is embedded within the human form of life. In a society that focuses on production, the principle 'from each according to their abilities, to each according to their needs' will always tip the scales in favor of abilities. Needs will be taken care of, at best, by charitable agencies. It is precisely the ancient democratic nature of consumption, that is, of need, coupled with its modern productivity that entails an epochal change in how we view the world. For as long as abilities have been distinguished from needs, the latter have always taken a backseat. But in a world where production is increasingly automated, needs—that which cannot be automated and constitutes the ultimate goal of production—become decisive. Indeed, they are the only thing that matters. In this sense, at a time when the Web seems to be interested not in what we do as bearers of strength, intelligence, and ability, but in what (rightly or wrongly) we desire, focusing on needs is not just the heart's desire but a fundamental economic law.

The idea that underlies twentieth-century welfare and has allowed the Left to socialize the surplus value of industrial capital was to consider saving and investment as two sides of the same coin. If we view capital as a whole, we must overcome the moralistic belief that those who put money in the bank are rewarded because they save. This is not the case: they are rewarded because they make money available for investment, thus supporting long-term consumption that represents the ultimate goal of all production of goods. Investment represents the royal road to achieve what—in an era of imperfect automation—constituted the fundamental objective of welfare: full employment. For this to happen, "the gay of to-morrow are absolutely indispensable to provide a *raison d'être* for the grave of to-day."[1] In other words, saving today is done only to spend tomorrow, and savings without spending is meaningless. If I put money into a mattress and this mattress is found centuries later, it was never a capitalizing gesture but rather an unconventional way to stuff a mattress. Similarly, **in twenty-first century welfare, consumption and production will be considered as the two faces of the same reality**. We produce for future consumption, and the only animals truly capable of consumption are human animals.

The possibility to create new value is precisely what sets Webfare apart from traditional welfare. The latter involved the fair allocation of existing value, thus demanding difficult choices (healthcare or social support?). Furthermore, in the long run, it could not shield against those forms of 'equality restoration' such as wars, in which humans become equal in destitution because they cannot share abundance. Wars, in fact, cannot be stopped by eliminating weapons. To argue, for example, that investing 2% of the global GDP by reducing military spending would

---

1   John M. Keynes, *The General Theory of Employment, Interest and Money* (London: Macmillan, 1936), 105f.

solve the environmental crisis is to propose a misguided option, both on factual and legal grounds. It is not feasible in practice and therefore not a solution. From a factual point of view, while we all wish for war to disappear from the theater of human affairs, I doubt that this wish has the remotest influence on the course of the world. From a legal point of view, even if humanity were to disarm itself in a unique historical event, leaving itself at the mercy of the bully of the day, it would be a regressive solution as it would affect existing value (a morally problematic value, but a value nevertheless) instead of creating new value. By contrast, Webfare can rely on a capital that did not exist twenty years ago, even though its content, the variety of human life forms, have existed as long as humans have. From time immemorial, humans have been making deals, consuming goods, cultivating interests, thereby manifesting specific forms of life. However, for a couple of decades now, these forms of life solidify automatically by transforming into data, which are not merely a reflection of human needs, thoughts, or behavior, but generate a new autonomous territory, a rich and promising one.

Acknowledgments

The writing of this essay was made possible by my research stay at the Center for Science and Thought at the University of Bonn in Spring 2023, as a Mercator Visiting Professor for AI in the Human Context. For their (practical and theoretical) support, I would like to thank the director of the Center, Professor Markus Gabriel, as well as Christiane Schäfer, the coordinator of the Mercator research project on "Desirable Digitalisation: Rethinking AI for Just and Sustainable Futures." I would also like to express my gratitude to all the members of the intellectual community at the Center who have been generous with their ideas, feedback, and inspiration. Among them, a special thanks to Dr. Ana Ilievska who not only translated and wrote the preface to this volume but also discussed and enriched it with her friendly and empathetic acumen as well as her intellectual wealth.

This book has been also written with heartfelt gratitude for the invaluable support provided by Cassa Centrale Banca, whose unwavering assistance has played a crucial role in bringing this work to fruition.

1. From The Tyranny of Merit to The Democracy of Need

As we shall see, this new and unhoped-for capital transforms into value what was once pure loss, i.e., consumption, the organism's ever-losing struggle to counteract entropy. As humanity's heritage, this new capital can now be intercepted, valorized, and redistributed among those in need, enacting in this way for the first time in human history a primacy of need over the tyranny of merit.[1] Such a shift constitutes an authentic and humanly effective way of reassessing all values. To understand the Web thus becomes a political act from digital warfare to Webfare, offering a unique chance to remedy the problems that have plagued humankind since the very beginning. How so? Certainly not for the reasons commonly cited when we speak about 'the Web,' still primarily considered a powerful communication tool. No, there is something deeper that must be brought to light. However, to do so, it is necessary to start from fundamentals that long predate the Web's appearance on the world stage.

---

1   Michael Sandel, *The Tyranny of Merit: What's Become of the Common Good?* (New York: Farrar, Straus and Giroux, 2020).

1.1 Nature and Society

Nature is unfair, at least for us who have the concept of 'justice,' since humans are born with different physical and cognitive gifts. Moreover, nature is not democratic. Why should it be? What does nature know about parliamentarianism or distributive justice? Humans are born ugly or beautiful, with limited or high cognitive abilities, and this disparity of conditions and views is reflected in conflicts, which are particularly sophisticated and layered, revealing humans to be infinitely more perverse and contentious than non-human animals. The claim that humans are all the same is far less credible than the claim that beavers are all the same because humans, more so than beavers, experience the pressure and speed of cultural evolution. **Culture and society, in turn, seek to mitigate injustices but introduce other even more odious ones** because they are created by humans rather than nature. Society, born not so much from the greed of the few but from the desire to remedy natural differences, succeeds to some extent. Unfortunately, in this attempt, it creates new disparities—such as the difference between haves and have-nots, and class inequalities—even more detestable than those generated by nature. Natural differences are a fact that cannot be blamed on anyone (it would be like reproaching a lion for not being vegan), whereas social differences are determined by humans fighting one another or, worse still, driven by the best intentions, the ones that pave the road to hell.

But how does one redistribute wealth and level differences if the goddess is not blindfolded? The concept of **meritocracy emerged** following the French Revolution as a reaction to traditional societies founded on advantage (or hardship) according to birth and was given its name not without a touch of polemic and irony. Its principle is foreshadowed by Napoleon's saying that in every soldier's knapsack, there could be hiding the baton of a Marshal of France. But the task is less straightforward than it appears, if only because not all knapsacks are equal, and merit is an aleatory and fickle notion that can range from the ability to solve problems to the skill of sweeping them under the rug. Even if a clear definition of 'merit' were firmly established, the fact remains that no one has truly earned their worthiness, be it in term of physical attractiveness, intelligence, or enterprise, just as they have not chosen their parents, the part of the world they were born in, nor the neighborhood or school district. And even when individuals do possess some agency over their own destinies, by and large, the die has already been cast.

So, if there is one lesson that we have learned from the past two centuries, then it is the need to pack away and stow in the attic the myth of **perfectionism**. This myth suggests that a person is born free and somehow finds themselves in chains, or that a person is born good but inexplicably becomes entangled in ethnic cleansing operations. We are not born full of goodness and altruism. Furthermore, it is entirely possible that we may never find ourselves in the material and cultural conditions that allow us to exercise these virtues. Therefore, it is primarily on the conditions that we must focus. The human animal, like any other animal, is not naturally predisposed to being either good or bad. However, unlike any other animal (because it is the only one capable of being educated), it must be placed in the conditions to be able to afford a conscience. Only then it can decide what moral temperament to give to its thinking and acting. These conditions do not fall from the sky but depend on how value is distributed in society. Contrary to what proponents of hunter-gatherer frugality or theorists of happy degrowth suggest, poverty does not produce virtue but oppression and war. And it is only growth—economic, social, and technological—that can guarantee the conditions that foster virtuous behavior.

1.2   Need and Consumption

But if we cannot rely on the dubious virtues of merit, or dream of a perfect origin to return to, on what can we base social justice? And what hope can we offer to the many who feel devoid of merit, yet are not immune to need? The proposal I bring forth involves precisely the **transformation of need, that is, of the great equalizer that unites humans, into a productive element** capable of generating new wealth. Thus, for the first time in the history of the world, we can implement the saying "from each according to their abilities, to each according to their needs." How? Let us start with the current situation. As much as merit is inherently undemocratic because it directly leads to the formation of an *elite*, need connects the human animal to the non-human animal and applies equally to all, much like death. There is no doubt, in fact, that the needs of billionaires and the vast resources they allocate to fulfill them, differ significantly from those of beggars. But in both cases, we are dealing with needs. Whereas, when we consider merit, particularly in the context of meritocracy, the billionaire's needs are hailed as the epitome of merit, while the beggar's needs bear the stigma of demerit, of one who has done everything wrong in life.

Above all, even if a significant portion of a magnate's merits can be automated through artificial intelligence systems, just as Hercules's feats were automated by the steam engine, the needs of a billionaire just as those of a beggar will never be replaced by a machine. There will always be some human in need, seeking solace in a tuna can or a trip into orbit, while no stone or machine will ever be able to cultivate a desire that even remotely resembles such needs (nor, indeed, can it experience that state so typical of organisms: desiring, striving, having intentions). The analogy between the needs of the rich and the poor (including, of course, the rich and the poor in spirit) does not merely concern the fact that "need" is something inconceivable for a machine or an inorganic being—stones do not have the need to fall to the ground; they simply obey the law of gravity, as Aristotle believed. It also concerns the fact that, **for a need to be fulfilled, in the specific case of the human form of life, a connection with one or more technical apparatuses is required**: the can that contains the tuna, the can opener, the rocket, the space capsule. In other words, insofar as the human lifeform is systematically connected with technology, human need is essentially rooted in consumption. This ranges from the most trivial material consumption to the highest form of consumption of cultural goods. Precisely because it is composed of organisms systematically connected with mechanisms (including symbolic and social apparatuses that qualify human nature as second nature), humanity is inherently ***technohumanity.***

Humans are organisms driven by needs and metabolic urgencies, just like any other organism. However, unlike any other organism, humans rely on technological supplements to compensate for their deficiencies. These enhancements began with flint and have now evolved into the indispensable role of silicon so important to the Web. Yet it must be clearly understood that nothing has changed in our essence: We are what we are not in spite of technology, but because of it. For instance, thanks to the keyboard mechanism I can write these words, leveraging decades of study and education, instead of running through the savannah while pursued by animals more formidable than ourselves without too many free decades (actually, not even a second) to dedicate to contemplation and learning.

This is a point that humanity tends to forget, especially when our attention is fixated on personal concerns or pressing global issues like the environment, war, and artificial intelligence. Amid such preoccupations, the topic of consumption may appear trivial or tangential, but this perception is unfounded. In truth, it is undeniably clear that **consumption is the element that shapes the very essence of the human form of life**, for better or for worse. If there were no competition for resources among humans, not only would conflict cease to exist (a timeless truth), but the looming specter of an environmental crisis would also disappear. After all, this crisis stems from the colossal effort by eight billion people upon our planet and its finite resources, and therefore has organic need as primary cause, starting with the most basic one of sustenance. This is the most conspicuous aspect.

But upon closer examination, consumption (and the needs that fuel it) emerges as a defining element of human existence, in contrast even to the world of machines. The latter, in fact, exhibit tremendous energy demands (the computer I am using to write these words, and then the system that will transmit them, consumes more energy than my fingers and brain). Yet, their need for energy is far less pressing than the one that I, as an organism, must deal with. After all, the computer can power down without any regrets or concerns, primarily because it lacks consciousness to cultivate such emotions and because it can always be revived, even after a week or a month or a year without energy supply. As for me, like any other organism, there is no such leeway: If I shut down, I simply cease to exist, and I do so permanently. The very fabric of the human life-form is shaped by this circumstance. **We have hopes, fears, and urgencies, precisely because we have needs, and these needs can ultimately be traced back to the need to respond to the demands dictated by our metabolism.**

During the early stages of Brexit, for instance, the looming food crisis in the UK caused by long queues of transport vehicles awaiting new customs controls became a genuinely serious and pressing issue. The gravity of these problems lay precisely in their impact on the urgency to fulfill organic needs. Neither the Metaverse nor ChatGPT would be seriously threatened by a food crisis, and both can patiently endure a power outage, provided, of course, that there are surviving humans interested in continuing to use Artificial Intelligence. We realize, thus, that the so-called virtual world to which we have supposedly graduated, leaving behind material existence, is far from being an *on-life* freely roaming the world like an aethereal spirit. Instead, it remains undeniably grounded in materiality, albeit in two different ways, depending on whether it concerns mechanisms or organisms.

Mechanisms are composed of matter and alimented by matter: Even the most immaterial of algorithms relies on a computer to run it, along with the often-scarce materials from which it is made, and, as in the case of Blockchain and AI in general, it requires enormous quantities of electricity. **Matter and its sustenance exert an incomparably stronger hold on organisms than on mechanisms, precisely because these are metabolic needs that cannot be postponed.** In both cases, beyond the allure of the virtual, the posthuman, and the immaterial, what dictates the law is need and its most tangible manifestation, namely consumption.

This is the crucial point that hasn't received enough critical attention, as for decades consumption has been subject to unfavorable scrutiny under the banner of capitalism, rising to the status of the eighth cardinal vice and serving as the synthesis of the other seven, from gluttony and greed to lust, with the possible exception of sloth (the abstention from action which might, perhaps, find its place within a program of happy degrowth). This is because consumption is immediately linked to 'con-

sumerism,' a byproduct of the industrial boom that shaped the upbring-
ing of the baby boomers and was subsequently passed down to later generations. Consumerism is a distortion as well as a hyperbole and a parody
of consumption—an unchecked, greedy, and wasteful binge.

**Granted, consumption can indeed be excessive, it is squandering,
and is driven by vanity. However, it is important to remember that consumption is the antithesis and, above all, the purpose of production. We
produce in order to consume**. Although it might seem more important
and noble to be a producer rather than a consumer, one can well imagine
a producer of low-quality, dangerous, silly, or futile objects just as one
can imagine a consumer who indulges not only in exquisite foods and
wines but also in works of art and philosophical theories. Most significantly, what is unimaginable is production in the absence of consumption. This is a pivotal consideration. At a time when AI seems poised to
supplant human endeavors across the board (albeit hypothetically), there
is one realm which it cannot infiltrate: the simple act of watching a film,
savoring a pizza, or yearning to attend a live concert.

Let us never forget this: **It is our needs, much more than our products, that make us who we are as humans, right from the start**. When
the newborn wants milk, this act does not only mark the beginning of
all future feeding behavior, but also the emergence of intentionality and
will, the seeds of consciousness. This becomes even more significant as
automation continues to render *homo faber* increasingly obsolete. While
humans are being replaced or become replaceable as bearers of strength,
patience, precision, and soon, in many cases, even of intelligence, there
is one area where no substitute can ever truly stand: consumption. Just
as the lofty philosophical saying reminds us that no one can die in place
of another, it is equally true that no one can eat on behalf of another. Our
needs and material activities form a fundamental economy detached
from income.[2] It is an unavoidable urgency that also presents an op-
portunity for a new economy based not solely on production but on the
capitalization of consumption.

---

2   Joselle Dagnes and Angelo Salento, eds., *Prima i fondamentali. L'economia della
vita quotidiana tra profitto e benessere* (Milano: Feltrinelli, 2022).

1.3 The Sorcerer's Apprentice

To achieve this, we need a sorcerer's apprentice: technology. Unlike other organisms that inevitably succumb to death, **only humans possess the unique ability to defer death through technology. This is precisely why humans are the masters of technology as it would be devoid of meaning without humans.** But if we were to ask someone whether technology is more akin to alienation or to revelation, the answer would likely lean toward the former; this not only because it is unclear how the concept of 'revelation' relates to technology, but because one of the first things that we are taught is that technology is alienating.

Now, upon closer examination, in order to argue that technique alienates us, we would have to accept a rather challenging premise: that human nature was created by God (be it the traditional deity or the new goddess, Mother Nature), and therefore endowed with virtues, intelligence, and vigor. Consequently, any departure from this state can only be seen as a decline. The once perfect being becomes imperfect, is expelled from the garden, gains awareness of good and evil, and resorts to a technological supplement represented by the fig leaf, which serves as a precursor to the myriad of other supplements that will accompany it on its newfound endeavor: work. Or, if we were to secularize the story, the Noble Savage becomes a liar driven by greed and a scheming oppressor. Consequently, as innocence fades away, he begins to seek solace in reinstating a sentimentalized imaginary past, for instance, through vacations immersed in a nature that is considered more natural the wilder it is, or in meticulously manicured French gardens. Yet technology and society persist even within these environments, ultimately leaving one with an overwhelming sense of alienation and exile from one's authentic self.[3] But isn't it paradoxical that those who claim to hold

---

3   In the U.S., Leo Marx has offered an acute analysis of the "American hero's" alienation in the face of technology: *The Machine in the Garden: Technology and the Pastoral Ideal in America* (New York: Oxford University Press, 1964), 364f: "In the end the American hero is either dead or totally alienated from society, alone and powerless, like the evicted shepherd of Virgil's eclogue. And if, at

life-and-death power over nature also perceive themselves as enslaved to technology? They see themselves as entrapped in a complex system of apparatuses which that very same weak and maladjusted animal has created to protect itself in a hostile environment? Once we recognize the implausibility of this tale, we can embrace an alternative narrative, one in which the notion of 'revelation' will seem far less obscure.

As we have long suspected—and as it becomes increasingly clear today through the transformations we experience—**there is no such thing as an inherent human essence, and the source of our humanity lies not within but outside of us, in technology and culture**. The natural state of being human is one of greater disadvantage compared to that of other creatures: lacking lethal claws or teeth, vulnerable to heat and cold more than any other animal, restless by nature, and lacking a natural habitat, everywhere we are ill-adapted. But from the moment a stick was used as a tool and the first flint was chipped to make a scraper, a distinct entity emerged known as the human being, something different from the non-human animal that it used to be. Among the various technologies, social technology is fundamental, and today it stands as the great new asset of mankind that must be understood and harnessed for the benefit of humanity alongside another technology: language. Language, along with the home and its furnishings, allows us to sit down and discuss our ideas about the origin of humanity instead of being chased by a saber-toothed tiger.

In this sense, technics has been our distinguishing trait compared to non-human animals since the very beginning. After all, why would humans alone possess such formidable advantages as sociability, language, and imagination? For as long as it was believed that God had fash-

---

the same time, he pays tribute to the image of a green landscape, it is likely to be ironic and bitter. The resolutions of our pastoral fables are unsatisfactory because the old symbol of reconciliation [the ideal of the middle landscape] is obsolete. But the inability of our writers to create a surrogate for the ideal of the middle landscape can hardly be accounted artistic failure. [...] The machine's sudden entrance into the garden presents a problem that ultimately belongs not to art but to politics."

ioned man in His image and likeness, it was not necessary to raise this question. But once it was raised, it spawned the dangerous tendency to search within humans, especially in their brains, for peculiar faculties that harken back to the world of Molière: Opium makes people sleep because it possesses the *virtus dormitiva*, humans speak because they possess neurons devoted to this function, just as they possess neurons assigned by the Supreme Clockmaker for reading, sociality, altruism, all the way to mathematics. If that were the case, humanity would not have ahead of itself an open-ended becoming but would be destined to develop latent potentialities within its grey matter, and temper the passions dictated by the amygdala and the lower layers of the brain. Now, this is not the case: **We are what we are much more because of what is outside of us than because of our natural endowments**. In practical terms, dolphins (with their larger and in some ways more capable brains than those of humans) have remained in the water. In such an environment, one cannot do things like lighting a fire, sharing stories around it, or deciding that it would be more reasonable to build a shelter to protect the fire from being extinguished, leading to an evolution through the systematic use of technological devices ranging from digging sticks to cell phones. **That is why the division between humanism and technology has never been justified, as humanism itself is a form of technology and technology exists only as a function of human consumption**. This is crucial. Consumption is not an accessory or extrinsic element of humanity; rather, it is its essence (if there is one), preceding language or thought precisely because, unlike the latter, it cannot be automated.

As I have shown elsewhere, this is where the Web comes in with a radical innovation: the valorization of humanity as *doc-humanity*, that is, as a producer of data and values rather than just material goods.[4] Let it be restated that for the first time in history we now have an apparatus that systematically and programmatically values humans not based on their merits but on their needs. What is even more remarkable is that it recognizes need as the most sublime merit of humans. It was already the case with the market: it doesn't matter whether what I produce is bought by a

---

4   Maurizio Ferraris, *Doc-Humanity* (Tübingen: Mohr Siebeck, 2022).

genius or a fool, as long as they buy it. But the Web enforces this principle not at the end of the process, but right from the start. The Web, and the automation and profiling it aims at, does not need to capture creativity or strength, beauty or intelligence, virtue, or wisdom, i.e., what makes humans different from other animals and from one another. Rather, it feeds on the continuous baseline that makes us equal even before death: the need, or more precisely the imbecility, the inherent lack that drives us to rely on technology. Therefore, it is necessary to recognize the value that humans generate on the Web, which would not exist without their needs. This empowers humans immensely in their relationship with technology and its present most conspicuous manifestation, the Web.

1.4 The Need for Theory

What I propose in this booklet is a theory, or at least a theoretical proposal, whose connection to the Web might not be immediately obvious. It has been argued that the need for theory would be rendered obsolete, what with the exponential growth of data, enabled by the ubiquitous recording capability of digital technology and the increased computational power of supercomputers.[5] Why bother with such imperfect shortcuts known as hypotheses and concepts, when we have a precise 1:1 map of the empire, and artificial intelligences that can swiftly survey it in every detail? And why should we invest our time in the pursuit of causal relationships that explain the events in the world, while exposing ourselves to the possibility of error, when it is far more lucrative and intellectually less demanding to entrust machines with the search for highly effective and irrefutable correlations?

Now, the exact opposite holds true: It is **precisely because of the immense growth of data and the fragmentation of knowledge and practices characteristic of our times that we need to develop a theory.** This

---

5   Chris Anderson, "The End of Theory: The Data Deluge Makes the Scientific Method Obsolete," *Wired*, June 23, 2008, https://www.wired.com/2008/06/pb-theory/

will allow us to navigate what would otherwise be a chaotic landscape not only from a cognitive point of view (this is the lesser evil), but from a historical and political perspective where it is a question of deciding the future course of humanity. This is based on the belief that all the data and many of the processes described in these pages, will soon undergo significant changes. Therefore, what I offer are the reflections of a humanist who has sought to engage with technologists to the best of his abilities but is painfully aware of his own limitations. Nevertheless, I am firmly convinced that **these continually metamorphizing processes and data find meaning only within a thoughtful exploration of the characteristics of the human form of life (including technology as its integral component).** Such an exploration can help shape, make sense of, and provide political guidance for the tremendous ongoing process.

Data, indeed, is a form of life, but interpretation—human interpretation—is indispensable in order to ascribe meaning to it. The presence of worked flint could be found throughout the Somme, but it took Boucher de Perthes to recognize them as traces of an ancient technology and way of life. Just **like the book of nature on the eve of the scientific revolution, the book of mankind only makes sense to those who study it with principles, concepts, and objectives. On its own, it is just a cacophony.** Galileo did not simply observe the world, but provided interpretations and reflections which he recorded in literal books. The principle applies to the vast book of the Web, awaiting its own Galileos, Torricellis, and Stahls. **That is why, in an age where human life can be captured in minute detail through data, the need for theory, understanding, conceptual frameworks, and interpretations is more critical than ever.**

The unfolding of such comprehension brings about epistemological fractures that demand our attention. Even before quantum physics, the statistical physics of Boltzmann and Maxwell introduced a probabilistic approach to the study of nature. The vast amount of information about the human experience comprising humanity's collective heritage enables the study of humans and societies to reach a level of approximation comparable to that of the natural sciences. It may even surpass it, considering that it delves into the mesoscopic and transparent dimension of human existence. This goes beyond a mere theoretical necessity; it is an ethical imperative. The need for theory also involves teleology, the attribution of purposes or objectives. As human beings with physical bodies, we have needs, pleasures, and goals, whereas machines lack them and, most importantly, derive them from us. I have no difficulty imagining a symphony composed by an AI. However, it is inconceivable for me to imagine an AI that desires to listen to a symphony and, in doing so, experiences pleasure, anguish, or exhilaration.

What distinguishes us as humans is precisely the fact that we are living organisms. We live, die, suffer, hope, fear, plan, despair. Our intelligence is intricately woven into the fabric of these experiences. Additionally, the certainty of our mortality imposes a sense of time and urgency upon our existence. We are not mechanisms that can be switched on and off like a light bulb. In contrast, "dying" is just a metaphor in the case of cell phones. If I bring my 'dead' phone to a technician, they can repair it. But if my grandfather passes away, he won't come back to life if I take him to the maintenance desk or to the hospital. And that is precisely why, from the very first day to the very last day of his life, my grandfather had urgencies, hopes, needs, and plans, while the cell phone (just as ChatGPT) simply executes pre-written programs.

To reject theory and resign ourselves to the dominion of technology (the two go hand in hand), would mean to relinquish our role as true architects of our own history. In this submission to technology and this renunciation of theory, humans succumb to the ancient mythologies such as that of the Golem, a clay giant who seeks to overthrow his master, or modern myths that proclaim technology as the sole master of history and humanity. Let us consider the matter from a different vantage point: A nineteenth-century office clerk who spent his entire day filling out documents required by administrative procedures, was he a slave to the bureaucratic machinery or to the human intention behind those procedures? Clearly, he was a human reduced to a mere machine, compelled to execute pre-written programs. The situation is far better now that we have computers perform such tasks. The need for theory (understanding) and teleology (the attribution of purposes and objectives) is a duty that can only be waived by a lethargic intellect. By rejecting them, we reject taking the responsibility that comes with being human.

2. From Analog to Digital

Let us start with the sorcerer's apprentice, the Web. **If it may seem that the Web, as a technical apparatus, is too insignificant to bring about a transformation that extends beyond the realm of the material into the spiritual and moral dimensions, it is because we have a limited concept of the Web.** We have, metaphorically speaking, a Ptolemaic image of the Web, focusing on its surface-level structures while overlooking its profound nature, not out of technological ignorance but rather a lack of philosophical attention. Today, 95 per cent of information is digital, and each year the volume of data doubles, surpassing the cumulative data of all previous history. Every internet interaction leaves a trace,[1] while sensors and cameras generate additional data that enriches the archive.[2] Algorithms not only monitor and evaluate human behavior but also comprehend our emotional states,[3] and even produce articles by drawing from the ever-expanding repository of recorded humanity.

It is precisely this vast archive that interests us as a form of capital because it represents a great theoretical novelty that demands our

1   Dirk Helbing, *Next Civilization: Digital Democracy and Socio-Ecological Finance—How to Avoid Dystopia and Upgrade Society by Digital Means* (Cham: Springer, 2021).
2   Shoshana Zuboff, *The Age of Surveillance Capitalism: The Fight for a Human Future at the New Frontier of Power* (London: Profile Books, 2019).
3   Markets and Markets, "Emotion Detection and Recognition (EDR) Market," 2022, https://www.marketsandmarkets.com/pdfdownloadNew.asp?id=233761

strategic attention. Merely a decade ago, it was said that financial capital would dominate the twenty-first century[4] and nobody suspected the emergence of documedia capital. The times have changed. With the Web capturing and transforming the myriad facets of human life into data, a new and unprecedented form of data capital has come into existence.[5] As a result, the explosion of recording that defines our era has fundamentally altered ontology by giving rise to a proliferation of social objects. We have an unprecedented wealth of documents, and their numbers are set to grow exponentially (arguably, the docusphere is destined to expand even more rapidly than the anthroposphere). **For the first time in history, social objects outnumber natural objects by an increasingly powerful and rapid progression.** These documents possess a unique characteristic.

While many of them (what I will define as 'semantic data') continue to be the result of a deliberate production process, a far greater volume of documents (which I will define as 'syntactic data') represents the simple and automatic record of human activity, primarily driven by consumption. As production becomes increasingly automated thanks to data interpretation, and enormous profits are derived from profiling, we are witnessing **a historic junction where consumption is more valuable than production.**

To truly grasp the extent of this transformation, we must shift our perspective from "the Ptolemaic Web," which primarily focuses on information and communication, to "a **Copernican Web**" that revolves around the concepts of recording and capitalization. Just as Voltaire famously remarked that the Holy Roman Empire was neither holy nor Roman, we come to realize that digital technologies are not merely ICTs

---

4   Thomas Piketty, *Capital in the Twenty-first Century* (Cambridge, MA: Harvard University Press, 2013).

5   "The Rise of Data Capital," *MIT Technology Review Custom + Oracle*, March 21, 2016, http://files.technologyreview.com/whitepapers/MIT_Oracle+Report-The_Rise_of_Data_Capital.pdf See also, Viktor Mayer-Schönberger and Thomas Ramge, *Reinventing Capitalism in the Age of Big Data*, cit.; Paul Sonderegger, "Data Hits Peak Metaphor," March 4, 2021, https://paulsonderegger.com/2021/03/04/data-hits-peak-metaphor/

(Information and Communication Technologies), as the acronym we still employ to refer to them misleadingly suggests. They are, in essence, neither purely information, nor communication, nor (as we shall see) simply technologies. They are, above all else about recording. This crucial distinction marks a radical departure from the past.

The Web is interesting precisely because it goes beyond communication and information-sharing and records the multifaceted tapestry of human life. This act of recording serves several purposes: as the basis for the development of algorithms and archives that fuel the automation of production through the mimicry of the forms of human life recorded on the Web; the optimization of distribution through analytical insights into our needs and behavior; as well as the profiling of social reality through the identification of the intricate correlations between consumption patterns, political inclinations, preferences, and predispositions of various kinds that do not concern individuals, as they may be cognitively less interesting. The focus is rather on ideal types. All of these transformations unfold within a space that stages the human comedy, or more precisely drama (δρᾶμα, i.e., 'action'), as it revolves around actions—sometimes tragic, often comedic, but mostly mundane in nature such as getting an Uber, booking an Airbnb, grocery shopping, or ordering a book.

As with the discovery of America, it is a case of *serendipity*. **If the digital realm has profoundly changed the world, it is due to a minimal and seemingly irrelevant technical feature. In the analogue world, communication took precedence, with recording being an occasional and separate endeavor requiring distinct tools than those used for communication.** Communication happened orally while recording involved the use of hands, pen, and paper. This is no longer the case. In today's digital realm, every act of communication generates a document, i.e., data. Rather than transporting us to a realm beyond our world, the Web introduces new objects—vast quantities of documents—into it, and that is why its impact is so decisive. Therefore, the radical novelty brought about by the Web is not the increase of information, but rather the automation of recording.

Traditionally, recording demanded effort, labor, and financial resources. Consequently, a significant portion of humanity's pre-Web
activities have left no trace. This becomes even more apparent when we
consider ancient civilizations where social acts were not recorded in
writing but rather preserved in forgotten rituals. Since the advent of
the digital, we forgot about those objects that required cassettes and
tape and which defined the childhood and youth of my generation. This
is not because, through some social miracle, recording has lost its significance (which would be impossible, as recording forms the bedrock
of social reality),[6] but rather because the fundamental characteristic
of the digital realm lies in the fact that every piece of information, in
order to be communicated, must first be encoded and thus recorded.
To designate the production/consumption of information by users, the
category of the "prosumer" has been exhumed,[7] but its resurgence is
both insufficient and anachronistic. It is not merely information that
is being produced but rather documents which, as we will see, in many
cases are *not* accessible to producers themselves.

For this reason, it seems more appropriate to introduce a fresh
term that fittingly captures this new status of documentality as the
vast archive constituting the social world: **documediality.**[8] In social
networks, communication is no longer confined to one-to-many type of
interactions but has expanded to encompass many-to-many exchanges,
and it has now even extended beyond the realm of the living (consider,
for instance, the progressive growth of accounts of deceased users,
which by 2070 may surpass the number of accounts belonging to the
living, although the reliability of such estimates remains uncertain).
Concurrently, and precisely because of the priority of recording, every
interaction with the Web for the purpose of accessing services or com-
posing messages produces an immense volume of documents that, in

6   Maurizio Ferraris, *Documentality: Why It Is Necessary to Leave Traces* (New York:
     SUNY Press, 2012).
7   Luciano Floridi, *Philosophy and Computing: An Introduction* (London and New
     York: Routledge, 1999).
8   Ferraris, *Doc-Humanity*, cit.

their raw form, possess minimal to no intrinsic meaning. However, when subjected to appropriate interpretation, these documents can acquire tremendous semantic value, thereby assuming political, scientific, social, and economic significance. We are thus witnessing the most efficient and powerful capitalization in history, a phenomenon that has not yet been fully appreciated except by U.S. libertarian platforms and Chinese communist platforms. And what drives this immense apparatus? Automation? Clearly not. Machines, in and of themselves, do not progress or generate value. Their value and products stem from the appreciation and needs of human beings. Therefore, consumption, which is essentially the human, is the alpha and omega of automation (currently) and economics (always).

The Web began producing data the moment it began recording every form of human life, including the most evident manifestation of need in the social world, namely consumerism, as well as all the various distinctive forms of human existence that arise in response to the different degrees of sophistication in meeting these needs.[9] **Consumption, which for hundreds of thousands of years simply used to vanish like tears in the rain, now, through recording, not only facilitates automation but also offers invaluable economic benefits through profiling.** Machines, however, do not know what humans want, how they behave, and what their needs, preferences, habits, and eccentricities are. As the production and distribution of goods increasingly fall under the purview of machines, which have, in the meantime, acquired the capacity to learn from experience, educating them about human life becomes a fundamental economic imperative. Moreover, even in cases where processes are not entirely automated, a deep understanding of consumption enables the implementation of a planned economy. The dream of Soviet five-year plans, which floundered because of the difficulty in predicting human

---

9   Suffice it to say that 4.7 billion people, accounting for more than half of the global population, owns a cellphone, not to mention that an immense number of sensors are interconnected in the network independently of cellphones. Estimates suggest that within the next decade, their count will reach a staggering 150 billion.

needs and behaviors, is now standard practice among capitalist companies.[10]

10   Leigh Phillips and Michal Rozworski, *The People's Republic of Walmart: How the World's Biggest Corporations are Laying the Foundation for Socialism* (London: Verso, 2019).

Before addressing the characteristics of the new capital that has emerged with the Web, it is important to acknowledge a network of interconnected spheres that form its premises. The first is the **ichno-sphere**, representing the realm of accumulated traces that humanity has capitalized on since its origins and that sets it apart from non-human animals. Then we have the **infosphere**, which predates the Web and emerged with the development of culture thousands of years ago. This sphere allows for the capitalization of knowledge beyond the experience of individuals. Next there is the **docusphere**, as old as writing itself, but that has been significantly enhanced, indeed transformed, through the digital revolution which transformed recording from a rare and costly activity to a ubiquitous and systematic process. However, the docusphere does not record everything indiscriminately; it is selective and captures those aspects of the human life form that hold relevance for the next sphere: the **anthroposphere**. It is this realm, the realm of human life, that is master over the docusphere and technology in general, even if humans, for various and often unfounded reasons, perceive themselves as its slaves.

I have already proposed elsewhere a detailed analysis of the fundamental spheres that comprise the Web,[11] and subsequently refined and expanded the spheres into a more comprehensive phenomenology.[12] Here, I will limit myself to a concise overview in order to show how the explosion of recording within the Web has brough about an ontological shift. It has transformed need, previously seen as mere loss, and consumption (the human manifestation of need), once considered mere waste, into the source of a new capital that can address the needs of an increasingly populous and needy humanity, while also generating value.

---

11   Ferraris, *Doc-Humanity*, cit.

12   Maurizio Ferraris and Guido Saracco, *Tecnosofia: Tecnologia e umanesimo per una scienza nuova* (Rome and Bari: Laterza, 2023).

2.1 Ichnosphere

What do the handprints on cave walls mean? The notion, somewhat naïve and tinged with superstition, that everything we do not understand must have a religious significance suggests that we are dealing with remnants of a ritual. But why not imagine a prehistoric mother telling her children "Stop it, can't you see that you're making a mess on the wall?" In both scenarios, we would be confronted with intentional traces. Further into the cave, food residues and arrowheads are unintentional traces, evidence of a bygone life. Moving closer in time, we have the pyramids and papyri adorned with hieroglyphics, codices and parchments, baroque libraries, and then those great centers of document production and distribution known as banks and registry offices, stock exchanges and major countries, newspapers and governments—all this for us today is the Web. *All this is capital, and nothing else.*

Before the Web and before recorded history, there is a more primordial and fundamental sphere, a metaphysical one that concerns a universally attested phenomenon, even beyond the technological realm although it represents one of its enabling conditions. This phenomenon is what I have sought to define as 'hysteresis,'[13] namely the survival and potential capitalization of an effect even after the cause has ceased to operate. In this framework, hysteresis is comprised of a range of functions associated with recording (and which I introduced in detail elsewhere[14]): **inscription**, at the ontological level, allows for something to be recorded thus escaping the transience of the event; **iteration**, at the technological level, allows for indefinite repetition of what is recorded, initiating a process of idealization and capitalization; **alteration**, at the epistemological level, refers to the possibility, though not necessarily the inevitability, of transformation through the process of iteration, whereby

---

13   Maurizio Ferraris, *Hysteresis: The External World* (Edinburgh: Edinburgh University Press, 2024).

14   Maurizio Ferraris, *Agostino: Fare la verità* (Bologna: il Mulino, 2022).

the quantitative becomes qualitative, giving rise to meaning; finally **interruption**, or the eschatological dimension, highlights the fact that every process has an endpoint and is meaningful only for organisms, such as humans, who possess a metabolic process that concludes with an irreversible interruption. Hysteresis is comprised of a set of operations that involve the genesis, structure, evolution, and fate of traces. Therefore, the sphere of hysteresis is called the 'ichnosphere,' viz., the sphere of traces (ἴχνος in Greek).

Recording happens when a trace is fixed in place. The principle of sufficient reason, valid for the natural cosmos, the social world as well as individual psychology, thus resonates with the phrase *nihil est sine hysteresis*, nothing exists without hysteresis. As in the case with black holes, there can be recording without matter, but matter cannot exist without recording. Now, the question "Why does something exist rather than nothing?" risks futility, as it originated during a time when the search for a primary cause of the universe appeared to be the essential task of science, philosophy, and theology. However, if we reframe the question as 'Why does something *persist* rather than nothing?' then even the question mark becomes superfluous. Everything that is exists because it is recorded, because it maintains a primary level of hysteresis thanks to which, with the Big Bang, the universe emerged from an original recording, a substance that was essentially memory. For instance, the words you are currently reading would not have been possible without a lengthy evolution that presupposes capitalization and transformation. Yet both you and I are inclined to see them as products of my thought, a mere verbalization of my thought, and that the computer is a mere tool to record and transmit them.

Once a trace is recorded, it can start undergoing **iteration**, the capitalization process typical of technology. In other words, the ichnosphere is the necessary, though not sufficient, condition for technology. The Big Bang, the scratch on my cell phone, the compounded interests of capital, language acquisition, the family history predisposing us to rheumatism, and the neuroses that compel us to approach relationships through patterns experienced in childhood—all these are manifestations of this idea: A medium preserves the trace of an action, temporally deferring its presence beyond the here and now of its production; but this deferral is not an ontological doubling yet, for it can only give rise to new (more complex and qualitatively distinct) objects when a trace is linked to another trace in a process of capitalization. What is can be not only accumulated (preservation is ontological) but also iterated (repetition is technological). The second step is therefore iteration: what remains can be repeated, generating capitalization and enhancement. To move from ontology to epistemology, one must traverse technology. Acts performed by technology are *synthetic acts*, synthetic judgments beings one of its subsets. In both the outcome is not derived from the analysis of premises: 12 does not arise from the analysis of 7 and 5, but rather from their sum, just as a statue does not emerge from the mere analysis of the marble of which it is made. The same holds true for the outcome of a battle, the success of a cake, the conclusion of a contract, the making of a promise. Synthesis—the result—is *a posteriori*, yet the conditions that make it possible are *a priori*, in the sense that they cannot be even minimally anticipated and understood through the mere analysis of form, actions, or materials.

Alteration is then a modification that can occur during iteration as in the transition from the quantitative to the qualitative, from sign to meaning. This process, as we shall see, plays a crucial role in the genesis of so-called 'big data.' Iteration can thus undergo qualitative changes as it occurs when *praxis* transforms into *poiesis*. The paradigmatic realm of alteration is epistemology, viz., the domain of what we know or believe to know, a reorganization of the known that leads us toward the unknown, a doing that becomes knowing, and more profoundly, a transition from what is merely mechanical to what is human, the result of the interaction between organism and mechanism.

Praxis has hysteresis, so to speak, behind itself for it consists in the iteration of gestures learned and perfected through practice. Poiesis has hysteresis behind and ahead of itself, with all the effects resulting from imitation and exemplarity. In this sense, the nature of the relationship between ontology and epistemology guaranteed by technology does not consist in top-down construction but in bottom-up emergence whereby epistemology emerges from ontology through technology, that is, from competence without understanding. At a certain point, iteration can turn into alteration, into the reconfiguration of a given, knowledge-independent field, which at a certain point, and following a technologically determined method, generates a meaning that was previously not evident: the butler is the murderer; the earth is round; Madame Bovary is a fictional character. Epistemology is the (not necessary but always desirable) result of the encounter between ontology and technology, between recording and iteration, that can give rise to something qualitatively different, namely, alteration. Iteration, in fact, is not only the possibility to guarantee the persistence of objects in space and time; it also allows for differentiation, the introduction of variation principles into repetition. Just think about species variation based on random mutations made possible by an enormous temporal extension and an even greater availability of material.

Every process has an end. And it is in this **interruption** that we recognize the *telos*: the progression comes to a halt, and meaning, purpose, and goal emerge. This final function of hysteresis concerns everything that is, but it has quite a peculiar significance for humans. Hysteresis is not an infinite process. Everyday experience shows that everything that is ends: mountains erode, stars explode, washing machines obey their fate of planned obsolescence, and organisms follow the road of everything that is flesh. This may seem disheartening, and indeed it is. However, upon reflection, the opposite would be worse. Not only would we face eternal boredom, but above all, everything would lose its meaning. Why? Because everything is what it is because it relates to organisms, to humans in our case, who, aware of the ticking clock and the final destination, produce all those things that make humans unique, at least in our own eyes. Only that which has an *end* can have an *end-goal*, as it is aware—if it is a professor—of the uniqueness of choices and the historicity of existence, and of the pressure of alimentary and vital needs, whether it is a professor or a duck.

2.2 Infosphere

Descending from metaphysics, we enter the sublunar world of cell phones and computers. Why do we buy them? Largely, to access information and services. The infosphere[15] is the visible face of the Web, where conspicuous phenomena occur, such as fake news or privacy threats, diverting attention from the underlying structure. The Web is often portrayed as consisting *only* of an infosphere, but the infosphere is merely the tip of the iceberg—an island of information gathering semantic capital no different (except for greater accessibility) from what can be acquired in any analogue environment, be it a print newspaper, a traditional library, an art gallery, an old television set or radio. The fact that analog and digital are interchangeable is evident from the systematic hybridization of analog and digital today. The capital formed in the infosphere consists of **semantic data**, of meanings that can be true or false like any other meaning. It is a capital that can be easily read without any special hermeneutic tools. As such, in terms of content it is no different from the analogue world except, as mentioned, for its greater accessibility: I can search for information right there on my cell phone instead of going to a library. Therefore, *nihil est in infosphera quod non fuerit prius extra infospheram*. In short, we have a mere digital doubling of things such as train schedules, libraries, newspapers, diary pages, and letters to pen friends, all available in analog format.

Once this is understood, it becomes clear that there is a misconception associated with the notion of the 'infosphere,' namely the idea of the Web as *collective intelligence*.[16] Admittedly, a library can metaphorically be called a 'collective intelligence' so there is no reason to view the Web differently. But the idea that an encyclopedia is much more knowledgeable than its most learned editors is swiftly contradicted by the fact that an

---

15   Alvin Toffler, *The Third Wave* (New York: William Morrow, 1980. See also Luciano Floridi, *The 4th Revolution: How the Infosphere is Reshaping Human Reality* (Oxford: Oxford University Press, 2014).

16   Pierre Lévy, *Collective Intelligence: Mankind's Emerging World in Cyberspace* (New York: Plenum Trade, 1997).

encyclopedia cannot read and thus knows nothing. The same applies to the Web. There is a wealth of information in a library, but the library is as ignorant as the shelves that hold the books. Again, the same applies to the Web. One can best examine the infosphere from three distinct positions: idealism, skepticism, and realism. **Idealism** arises from the hypostatization of the infosphere, called upon to represent the totality of the Web, which is in turn identified with the totality of the world. This is summarized in the thesis that the informational is real and the real informational.[17] If this were the case, the digital revolution—unlike the other revolutions it is often compared to[18]—would, in fact, have the features of a philosophical restoration, returning us to Berkeleyan idealism. For Berkeley, only ideas existed, and in the hypothesis of the infosphere, only information exists.

Now, as it has been authoritatively pointed out,[19] we have two possible approaches. On one hand, we can embrace an information theory akin to the one used in physics and speak of information in the same breath as mass and velocity. However, this raises questions about why we have entered the infosphere precisely at this moment and why we specifically refer to it as the 'infosphere' rather than the 'energosphere,' 'massosphere' or 'tachisphere.' On the other hand, we can take a more conventional understanding of 'information.' In this case, there are two scenarios: either we acknowledge that information is merely a part of reality, as it has always been, recognizing the distinction between epistemology and ontology, thereby negating any need to argue that we live within the infosphere; or we can assert the equivalence of the real and the informational, affirming that ontology and epistemology are identical and falling into the trap of a transcendental fallacy by equating being with being known: *esse est concipi*. Unless we wish to embrace a doctrine

---

17 Luciano Floridi, *The Logic of Information: A Theory for Philosophy as Conceptual Design* (Oxford: Oxford University Press, 2019).

18 Floridi, *The Fourth Revolution*, cit.

19 John R. Searle, "What Your Computer Can't Know," *The New York Review*, October 9, 2014.

that boasts few conscious defenders[20]— even though it served as the implicit foundation and thus the intrinsic fragility of postmodernism in the last century[21]—we must view the infosphere not as a new world that envelops and replaces the old, but rather as an interactive realm that has existed since time immemorial and has now become readily accessible through the Web.[22]

Information is a primary good since it is in knowledge that our competitive advantage over non-human animals lies. Unfortunately, knowledge has the frustrating characteristic of potentially being false. This is where the presumed advantage turns into ruinous disadvantage. We will never see a beaver burned at the stake by the Inquisition or ruined by smoking. Neither the beaver nor any other form of life, except for humans, can conceive the idea that ontology, or what exists, depends on epistemology, or what we know or believe to know. Since Kant, however, this aberrant conception is widespread among human animals. The first step forward in epistemology must therefore involve abandoning the conviction that what exists is identical to what we think exists.

One version of the infosphere linked to **skepticism** or the suspicion syndrome is the hypothesis of "surveillance capitalism."[23] The aim of market knowledge through data is not only about leveraging data to boost sales but also about standardizing people's tastes and preferences. The true power of the Internet giants would then lie in their ability to induce questions in users before providing the desired answers. However, it is unclear how any commercial benefit could emerge from such

---

20   John Foster, *The Case for Idealism* (London: Routledge, 1982).

21   I discussed this perspective at length in my *Manifesto of New Realism* (New York: SUNY Press, 2014).

22   Unlike Teilhard de Chardin's "noösphere," or Frege's and Popper's "third world," the infosphere does not represent an entirely autonomous domain of abstract entities. Instead, it takes on a humbler role, as Alvin Toffler, its originator, has aptly described it—an expansive sphere of technological possibilities that enables knowledge dissemination, self-expression, and entertainment. Cf. Pierre Teilhard de Chardin, *The Vision of the Past* (New York: Harper & Row, 1967).

23   Zuboff, *The Age of Surveillance Capitalism*, cit.

uniformity in consumption. Conversely, there is nothing more commercially profitable than the freedom, or rather the diverse and endlessly evolving 'unpredictability' of human tastes, which continually unveil untapped commercial frontiers.[24] As for skepticism, a final point of paramount importance and deserving thoughtful contemplation arises: the same allegations that platform capitalism faces as surveillance capitalism, back in the 1960s were aimed at the 'hidden persuaders' of the society driven by advertising, conventional mass media, and the age-old industrial capitalism—all this well before we had the faintest glimpse of the Web's advent.

Finally, from the standpoint of **realism**, semantic capital (with its wealth of content and services) provides a powerful incentive for humans to access the Web and obtain information while simultaneously generating a surplus of information. It is a polarizer of needs rather than a receptacle of ideas. The primary function of semantic capital is that of an alluring magnet, aiming to provide compelling reasons for humans to access the Web. As such, it does not guarantee truth but is solely focused on arousing interest. It is therefore not surprising that the infosphere is the breeding ground for post-truth, precisely because it is the realm of attractions, opinions, insinuations, and social exchange. But this does not mean in any way that the polarization typical of online interactions makes post-truth an entirely novel phenomenon in world history. As it has been rightly observed,[25] post-truth is merely magnified and empowered by the technical characteristics of the new tool, the great attractor

---

24   In 1919 Keynes wrote *The Economic Consequences of Peace*, where he warned against the severity of the conditions on those who lost the war, though his advice went unheeded. Nonetheless, his work laid the foundation for the Marshall Plan. Today we would be happy if a revived Keynes wrote *The Economic Consequences of Freedom*. The spirit is by definition free, without necessarily being wise, good, or intelligent. That is why, if freedom is an obstacle to planned economy, the platform economy recognizes that nothing is more profitable than freedom as an expression of the infinite and often irrational forms of human life.

25   Cf. Fabio Paglieri, *La disinformazione felice: Cosa ci insegnano le bufale* (Bologna: il Mulino, 2020).

of human curiosities, vices, and virtues. This, I believe, confirms my fundamental thesis about the infosphere: far from constituting the entirety of the Web, it motivates humans to access the Web by providing high or low-quality services, truth or post-truth, all free of charge. However, once humans are drawn into the infosphere, they produce an enormous amount of data within the docusphere. It is at this stage that the platforms begin acquiring documents which, if compared with billions of other documents generated by humanity as a whole and interpreted correctly, produce inestimable value in terms of automation, profiling, and advertising revenue.

2.3 Docusphere

The docusphere is the ocean in which the islet of the infosphere rises. It is the domain where the acts of humanity are registered and capitalized upon, transforming into data that compose what I will later define as 'the human heritage.' This is a social capital that mankind has always produced, but in today's era, it produces it in quantities unprecedented in the past. The true revolution brought about by the Web does not merely lie in the possibility to express our ideas, whether right or wrong, but rather in the fact that, as we express ourselves or simply engage in activities like reading, scrolling, walking, looking for restaurants or hotels, or seeking navigational guidance, these actions are meticulously recorded. Once they are recorded, they can be compared with the acts of millions of other humans, shedding light not on the ethereal skies of our thoughts and beliefs, but on the tangible soil of our actions and deeds.

Once we step into the docusphere, within the vast sea of the Web, it becomes imperative to distinguish between **semantic and syntactic data.** Semantic data can be comprehended given the necessary cultural framework (such as knowing Hungarian when reading a Hungarian Wikipedia entry), whereas syntactic data (geolocation, contact history, and the broader scope of what is known as "metadata") only acquire meaning through correlations with billions of other data points—a task that currently only large platforms can handle. The science required to understand semantic data is available to any educated person, while comprehending syntactic data necessitates access to unfathomable volumes of information and the possession of immense computing power—privileges currently enjoyed by only a handful of big players. Currently, it is primarily syntactic data that generates surplus value. More concretely, the docusphere is the structure wherein **syntactic capital** is generated. This is a new form of capital on par with financial capital in its capacity to birth new digital products and services. However, syntactic capital has its own set of rules.[26] Unlike financial capital, it does not require a deliberate intention of capitalization; rather, we produce syntactic capital while engaging in other activities. From this perspective, the analogy of data as the "new oil"[27] is misleading for two significant reasons.

First, data is different from oil in that it is renewable energy—much like ideas, data can be shared and reused to our heart's content. Second, oil was formed millions of years ago through the decomposition of dinosaurs, rendering it a resource for which no entity can claim restitution. In contrast, we actively produce data ourselves and possess every right to demand that it be returned, not so much to us as individuals (individual data has little value) but rather to humanity, which stands as the true rationale behind the capitalization of this newfound value. Like the Native Americans facing the conquistadors, we often deem the exchange between syntactic data (gold) and semantic data (colored beads) advantageous or at least equitable. But if the natives engaged in such trading practices because they belonged to a culture different from the one of the conquistadors, we have far fewer justifications—unless we want to invoke the *ignava ratio*, the lazy reasoning that leads us to believe that the

---

26   Paul Sonderegger, "Three Things You Should Know About the Hidden Data Economy," *Paul Sonderegger* (blog), November 23, 2020, https://paulsonderegg er.com/2020/11/23/three-things-you-should-know-about-the-hidden-data-ec onomy/

27   "Data Is the New Oil," coined by mathematician Clive Humby. See Michael Palmer, "Data is the New Oil," *ANA Marketing Maestros*, November 3, 2006, h ttps://ana.blogs.com/maestros/2006/11/data_is_the_new.html

most interesting aspect of the Web is the effortless access to transparent information that it grants us. The politically decisive aspect in this context is therefore to recognize the processes of surplus value formation.

In the realm of communication technologies such as the traditional telephone, users paid for a service (often too much because of monopolistic practices) and, as soon as they received it, that was the end of the transaction. The telephone company would collect the profits and try to reinvest them for further gain. By contrast, within the domain of recording technologies, such as the cell phone, when we make phone calls or perform searches free of charge, it merely marks the beginning of an immense capitalization process for the platform. The platform records the metadata (far outnumbering the information we received: the time, day, search location, personal details, etc.), thereby assuming ownership through primary accumulation. These records are subsequently compared to billions of other users' data, facilitated by technological and conceptual tools. The result are profiles that can be used for automation and distribution purposes, or can be sold, generating profits that surpass those of traditional stock investments, primarily because, let us recall, they were acquired for free.

But why do we provide data for free? Because of a **capturing process.** While I search the Web for evidence that the Earth is flat and the moon made of cheese, I am unwittingly divulging valuable information about the behaviors of flat-Earth proponents. The platform will use this data to sell me books on my favorite topics (if it is an American platform) or send me to a reeducation camp (if it is a Chinese platform). European platforms, empowered by the data portability law, could employ this treasure trove of information to promote a new well-being and social justice, perhaps ultimately mitigating the reasons that lead individuals to visit flat-Earth website in the first place. Cameras, telephones, smart eyeglasses and watches, and, of course, the trusty old computers meticulously record every act, glance, desire, need, spoken or written word, our every taste and disgust, stroke of genius as well as moments of sheer idiocy. Their purpose is not necessarily to control us and for good reasons: we are not that interesting as individuals. What truly matters are our patterns of conduct because the only way to serve humans and at the same time replace them is by knowing how they behave and what they want, and we have never possessed such profound insight into this as we do now. Our identities, political opinions, virtues, and vices are only of interest to our neighbors and the government, but certainly not to commercial platforms. What they are interested in is behavioral data: our whereabouts, air travel routines, preferred restaurants, and how often we visit specific websites. Their objective is not to scrutinize the abyss of our inner selves but to unveil correlations and general patterns, the continuous bassline and enduring tapestry of human life.

Given this state of affairs, **it becomes crucial to recognize the inequality in the relationship that currently exists between the paradigmatic form of technology (internet platforms) and the users.** By immersing ourselves in the infosphere, we can find out when the next flight to Madrid is, which is useful. However, the platform, which unlike me has access to the docusphere, learns how many individuals have searched for that information, where they were, what they did before, and what they will do afterwards. This enables the platform to compare the data with millions of other searches, providing insights not into the present but into the future. In essence, online platforms obtain profiles that, in this case, enable an airline to ensure consistently full flights. This economic advantage motivates the airline to pay the platform for the data we freely provided. Thus, the production of value is exploited, involving children and the elderly, the employed and unemployed, rulers and beggars, who, in exchange for free information and services, relinquish data that are of infinite value to those who possess the means to capitalize on them.

In light of these circumstances, our task is twofold. On the one hand, and in the critical spirit of humanistic knowledge, we must **recognize the surplus value** produced by humanity, often unconsciously, on the Web. On the other hand, in line with the practical function of technological knowledge, we must identify the tools that will allow us to achieve a **fair redistribution of this value**, benefitting the many. But where can we find the leverage point to overturn the balance of power? A simple reflection unveils the answer: **the Web will vanish the moment humanity ceases to exist. Therefore, its existence is fully contingent upon humanity much** like viruses depend on living organisms. This circumstance forms the basis for a fair use of surplus value. The human being, as a living being systematically connected to a mechanism, has never been as important as it is today.

While metaphysics, at least in its traditional misinterpretation, seeks to transcend physics, the metaverse promises an escape into the virtual while collecting information about what is supremely physical and tangible: our skin, our eyes, our hands. Never before has the so-called "virtual age" been imbued with such palpable reality. Only in the age of Artificial Intelligence have we truly grasped how essential natural intelligence is in conferring purpose and meaning. And this is not because natural intelligence is inhabited by a spirit that transcends the calculations of machines, but because it is embodied within an organism, a living system with its urgencies and mortality.

2.4 Antroposphere

The very possibility of a docusphere is dependent on the anthroposphere, that is, the circumstance that, in the absence of human users, the entire process of capitalizing on consumption within the docusphere would lose its *raison d'être*. We can be sure that a beaver will never try to access the internet for the very same reason that it won't use a shovel or wear a hat. Accordingly, it will never provide information about its way of life, its preferences, its deep motivations, and how exactly it builds dams. However, unlike beavers, humans provide the Web with a wealth of information about themselves, all meticulously documented within the Web's archives and reflecting their specific and diverse linguistic playfulness, aspirations, and aberrations. The interaction between the anthroposphere and the docusphere engenders a capital far superior to both industrial capital (increasingly facilitated by machines trained in the ways of humans) and financial capital (that merely speculates on the future hopes of a minuscule fraction of humanity). This because documentary capital, the data accumulated in the docusphere through sheer human activity, represents the most accurate portrait we currently possess of humanity's real present and, over the years, of its past. This new capital will outline a natural and social history of humans that, if studied adequately, stands unparalleled not only in economic terms but also in the purely theoretical realm of the Delphic "know thyself."

Human capital is, in a proper sense, the recording of human life as such in all its infinite variations. Yet, for now, the prevailing notion is that machines employ human contributions perfunctorily, albeit indispensably: whether explicitly, such as in microtasks aimed at enhancing the Web's efficiency,[28] or implicitly, as users help enhance image recognition systems through CAPTCHA,[29] or even through self-learning enabled by sophisticated digital technologies that manage and monitor labor. But these are mere surface effects of a deeper, radical reality that, if understood, holds great promise—the production of value by humans merely by virtue of being human. The point to be grasped and valued is another: Useless as appendages of shovels, lathes, and typewriters, humans are irreplaceable as appendages of knives and forks, cinema, concerts, novels, and countless other less commendable and yet exclusively human forms of entertainment.

To discover the value of human capital and draw the logical consequences for the benefit of the few has been the great advantage of commercial platforms. It is now up to us to draw the political consequences for the benefit of the many—civilians and military personnel, old and young, parents and children, pacifists and warmongers, geniuses and fools)—who deposit their interests, desires, hopes, and, above all, the silent acts and facts of their lives into the universal archive. One could certainly observe that there are poorer individuals than those who merely possess data. They are the victims of the *digital divide*, unable to reap its benefits and, most significantly, excluded from history because they do not generate data that renders them politically,

---

28   Amazon Mechanical Turk, https://www.mturk.com/
29   Acronym for "Completely Automated Public Turing Test to tell Computers and Humans Apart."

socially, and economically significant or interesting.[30] This amplifies the discriminatory potential of big data.[31] In response, I emphasize that the interest of commercial companies lies in extending access to its maximum, not because they want to diminish the digital divide out of humanitarian motives, but for political and economic reasons. The most glaring manifestation of this process can be observed in Africa where American and Chinese companies engage in a battle to make the vast quantities of data produced by one and a half billion individuals accessible through massive infrastructure investments.

30   Mark Andrejevic, "Big Data, Big Questions: The Big Data Divide," *International Journal of Communication* 8 (2014): 1673–1689, p. 17.

31   Maddalena Favaretto, Eva De Clercq, and Bernice Simone Elger, "Big Data and Discrimination: Perils, Promises and Solutions. A Systematic Review," *Journal of Big Data* 6: 12 (2019), https://doi.org/10.1186/s40537-019-0177-4

3. From Artificial Intelligence to Natural Intelligence

No machine, nor any non-human animal, produces value. Value is a primary production, wherein humans ascertain what is deemed valuable. Humans not only serve as the origin but also the ultimate purpose. For this reason, **I propose replacing the syntagm "human capital" with "human heritage" to emphasize that humans are not merely the replaceable instruments of production and distribution, but rather the ultimate aim and meaning of all that transpires in the world.** This is not an affirmation of aentrism: the planet does not need us to save it, and life will continue to flourish after the last human disappears. But after that disappearance, it will no longer make sense or be of interest to discuss those minuscule matters regarding the universe that are so important to us: truth, falsehood, value, love, history, hope—essentially, the distinctive human heritage. If there are goods and services, it is only because there are humans; if they possess value, it is because the world is populated not only by viruses, beavers, and processors, but also by organisms that, unlike viruses, beavers, and processors, satisfy their needs through a cooperative system we refer to as 'economy' and 'society.'

3.1 What Is Life?

Let us approach the issue in a manner that avoids treating life as a metaphysical and tautological entity, viz., as a driving force or a vital impulse, as it was the case in the philosophies of life between the nineteenth and twentieth centuries. Instead, we can observe that the soul, the vessel of organic life, encounters an absolute and insurmountable boundary known as "death." This boundary is absent in inorganic life as well as in the non-living matter that is the predominant component of the universe. It is also absent in the ubiquitous mechanisms within the human form of life, which, as mentioned, systematically intertwines organic and mechanical life. Mechanisms merely imitate the distinctive properties of organic life in a sequential manner but are devoid of genuine development and, most importantly, of a definitive end or cessation. There is a unique quality in life that prevails over mechanisms, however often we are wrongly inclined to consider ourselves as slaves to machines. The crux of the matter lies in the fact that **will, or that which confers meaning on moral action and makes it possible, finds its foundation precisely in our organic basis as non-human animals and in its connection not with the realm of ends but with the mechanical supplements that define us as human animals.** The value of life has never been as apparent as it is on the Web, especially at the tumultuous boundary between the anthroposphere and the docusphere. In fact, to ask it with Schrödinger, what is life? The shadow of a fleeting dream or the struggle of metabolism against entropy? It is both: an essential principle, the living as opposed to the dead, the ζωή, and that which is experienced subjectively as a direct experience, the life we live, existence, the βίος.

In both cases and as previously mentioned, **the distinction between automaton and soul lies in the irreversibility of metabolism, a characteristic of the soul. It is an absolute on/off that differs radically from the serial on/off pattern proper to mechanisms.** Here is the point: What makes an organism have intentions while a mechanism merely receives them? Trivially, the fact that when a mechanism stops working, it can be repaired, whereas when an organism comes to a halt, it does so permanently. This fundamental distinction accounts for the fact that organisms, unlike mechanisms, have urges, volitions, and emotions. Imagining a bored or scared computer is impossible not only because the computer does not know it is bored or afraid (sometimes it happens to us too) but because if it knew, it would also know that these feelings are unfounded: a computer has all the time in the world and all it needs is an update. This difference between on and off (organism) and the series of on/off, on/off, on/off (mechanism) applies to all animals, human and non-human alike.

Obviously, we are free to entertain the idea that our emotional frailties are not exclusive to humans and that automata (such as the replicants in *Blade Runner*) or superhuman beings akin to Greek gods could exist,[1] identical to us in every aspect. Such speculations are not illicit, as long as we acknowledge that they belong to the realm of fiction or myth. Yet, this is precisely why our forms of life have suddenly assumed such importance—they are unique. In *Existentialism Is a Humanism*, Sartre wrote that "we are on a plane where there are only men," leaving one to ponder which plane exactly he was referring to. Less than fifty years later, the clarification arrived: the plane is the Web, the great repository of human forms of life. **The anthroposphere, as the world of human life, that is, of the organism systematically connected to the mechanism, is therefore the foundation of the docusphere, which would not exist without humans and their forms of life.** On the level of the anthroposphere, we witness a twofold movement: on the one hand, the Web (in line with technology's basic tendency) is increasingly gravitating towards the organism, toward life as a genetic phenomenon of technology that holds significance only for a living being; on the other hand, that living being, which from its very inception has been intricately linked to technology and which precisely for this reason qualifies as "human," is increasingly gravitating towards the mechanism.

Let us recall what has just been said. Humans, like all organisms, have an internal purpose—metabolism as a struggle against death—resulting in only two states, on or off. When off, it remains so permanently. Unlike automata, which exhibit an evident external teleology (viz., they are means to an end), organisms are ends in themselves. The simple automaton, the tool, may break, but it can always be repaired or replaced. Complex automata are programmed for the longest possible series of

---

1   Martha C. Nussbaum, *The Fragility of Goodness: Luck and Ethics in Greek Tragedy and Philosophy* (Cambridge and New York: Cambridge University Press, 1986).

on/off cycles (traffic lights, internal combustion engines, computers) and the more intricate the process, the more the automaton reveals itself appropriate to its etymology (*automaton*, moving by itself). Nonetheless, this ideal tendency remains unrealized, for a complete movement necessitates an internal purpose while the automaton's purpose is externally motivated, for instance, by the soul that sets the home thermostat.

This circumstance constitutes the foundation of the superiority of humans over machines from an axiological standpoint, as **it is humans who confer value and meaning upon machines and tools. Alarm clocks and frying pans have explicit and unequivocal purposes: they are *made to* respond to the needs of organisms; humans—as mere organisms—are *made for* nothing more than sustaining themselves and deferring death**. But it is precisely through the encounter with mechanisms and the social world that those organisms assume their humanity. At this juncture, they discover that they are not solely *made to* live like brutes (merely following their internal purpose) but are also *made to* pursue an external purpose, the ideal of perfection. Such purpose was not part of their organic constitution but emerged from interactions with fellow humans and the highly sophisticated technologies of language, writing, and culture. In the human world, organisms interweave with the system of mechanisms and with that great machine that is society. Unlike non-human animals and just like a technical apparatus, external transcendent purposes are generated in the human animal through education.

3.2 The Techno-Anthropological Circle

This fundamental nexus constitutive of the human forms a **techno-anthropological circle: humans attribute external purposes to mechanisms (including the overarching mechanism of society), which in turn have a feedback effect on human organisms and shape the specific nature of humans, namely the second nature that we acquire through technology and culture.** This circle embodies both capitalization and value creation. The ongoing revolution is the greatest manifestation of this transformative cycle (the greatest known thus far), and it should not be underestimated, as neglecting its significance would leave us ill-equipped to address any resulting crises. For indeed, throughout history, humanity has always distinguished itself from mere animality by embracing technological apparatuses. These supplements that remedy our organic deficiencies are also forms of appropriation and capitalization. The time invested in producing a technical apparatus, regardless of its complexity, is time saved and repaid through the performance of the technical apparatus. Therefore, technology and capital are synonymous and should be comprehended as such. Those who, even with the best intentions, advocate for a return to a world devoid of technology and capital, offer us an ambiguous gift: a brief, miserable, brutal, monotonous life that, to make matters worse, is profoundly inauthentic.

To become human means to develop increasingly sophisticated technologies. If we have accurately gauged the historical trajectory we have followed so far, it becomes indisputable that we are becoming more human with each passing day. From the outset, human nature has been a second nature—the result of the interplay between organisms and mechanisms, soul and automaton. The development of the automaton is the revelation of the soul, of what we are, both in the extensive history that lies behind us and hopefully promising future that lies ahead. This process of capitalization is boundless and should remain so unless we choose to sign the date and time of humanity's demise. I refer to the whole of humanity and the progress that defines it as such, and not to individual humans, who, unfortunately, are only slightly less ephemeral than fruit flies, and whose passage on the world stage is always that of an extra. **Those who speak of the "limits of development"[2] often fail to consider that these are intrinsically tied to the brevity of life itself. It is futile and presumptuous to ask humanity to impose limits on itself when these limits are already insurmountably imposed by its organic nature.**

---

2   Donella H. Meadows, Dennis L. Meadows, Jørgen Randers, and William W. Behrens III, *The Limits to Growth* (New York: Universe Books, 1972).

The opposite of degrowth is capitalization. **The great misunderstanding about capital is that it exclusively refers to industrial or financial capital (with the latter as the degeneration of the former) when, in fact, "capital" is the umbrella term for any form of accumulation of skills. Therefore, civilization as a whole must be viewed as a process of capitalization. The choice we have is not between capital and the absence of capital, but between just and unjust forms of capitalization.** It is important to emphasize that "capital" does not necessarily mean greed but is a process of accumulation of knowledge, know-how, and power. In other words, it is what we call "civilization." To form capital is to defer the present use of goods or resources with a view to greater benefits in the future. Learning a new technique, accumulating assets, and achieving personal merit are all forms of capitalization.

Capitalization, as the product of a historical and social structure, is humanity's fundamental resource that underpins the very foundation of ethics. For moral values, just like monetary ones, exist only within a system. Hence, there is no one single "capital," let alone *the* capital, but a multitude of capitals engaged in relentless competitions with some surpassing others in significance and benefit. Capital's true value lies in its ability to leverage the resources of hysteresis—to save, accumulate, and, most importantly, reinvest. For **this is the great secret of capitalization: Once an event is recorded, it becomes an object that can be iterated, allowing for a conservation of energy and an increase in possibilities. The effects of this process are much more evident in cultural and general human spheres than in the financial domain.** Furthermore, capitalization does not involve privatizing and sequestering something from the public domain, quite the contrary: it involves sharing and diffusion. This is manifest not in financial capital but in the vast common capital formed by technology, culture, and language. It is the cumulative result of these acts of recording and iteration that has shaped humans into what they are today.

3.3 Natural Intelligence and Artificial Intelligence

Intelligence, whether natural or artificial, is the ripest fruit of capitalization. Natural intelligence resides within a body while artificial intelligence within a machine, or, more precisely, is the machine itself. This makes all the difference: organisms, whether human or animal, have needs, desires, fears, enabling them to strive for power. It is therefore not surprising that there are hierarchies of dominance and subordination within packs of jackals or department councils, whereas it would be difficult to conceive of a cell phone giving orders to a thermostat without human interference. Let us dispel the specters. A stick, as a simple machine, offers great versatility in its potential uses (lever, club, javelin) and the variety of users (human, monkey, beaver). A plow is already much more reliant on a human user but, in return, during the act of plowing, it enables the human to become an integral part of the technological complex on equal footing with the plow and, if fortunate, with the ox. The same can be said of an assembly line. In contrast, the quintessential machine of the twentieth century, the automobile, depends on humans only for directions. More importantly, the smartphone, the quintessential machine of the twenty-first century, is entirely dependent on how we use it and holds no meaning outside of that use. Finally, the essence of the universal machine, the absolute machine, namely artificial intelligence, is the pure recording and processing of human life forms. AI feeds exclusively on human blood but, unlike vampires, it has no urgency, no need, and no drive to do so: The Web will never come looking for us unless we look for it, unless we turn on the machine.

In light of what has been said so far, we must debunk the myth that automation turns us into automatons. In fact, when the available technologies are not advanced enough, it is even necessary to resort to a form of mechanization of the human. For instance, eighteenth-century treatises on the art of war outline systems aimed at transforming soldiers into components of a great mechanism capable of carrying out a series of maneuvers with precision. The same applies to Fordism, which intensifies the human-machine relationship albeit with the notable difference that it simplifies the human tasks and consequently makes them more tedious and alienating. So far, the evolution of technology has always required the automation of the human. However, **as technology becomes capable of replacing humans in functions beyond mere physical strength and precision, it is imperative to ensure that humans become more human.** Humans are of particular interest precisely because of their humanity, because machines do not know how humans behave but are sophisticated enough to record these behaviors and learn from them.

What we call "humanity" arises from the encounter between an internal purpose (that of an organism) and technological products endowed with external purposes, which, in the case of human animals, become defining factors of their essence. A gorilla without a stick is still a gorilla, and the first human, when wielding a digging stick, was still an anthropomorphic ape. Our ancestors probably oscillated for millennia between occasional and systematic uses of technical devices. However, humans only emerged when systematic use prevailed. The sophistication of technological apparatuses, extending beyond mere tools to include symbolic structures like language and social objects from basic kinship relationships to quantum physics, led humanity to become the defining feature of those natural objects, namely humans, who, through technology, become social objects. It is within this context, as a consequence of an emergent process unfolding as a continuation of natural evolution, that humans became subjects, viz., that human organisms transitioned from being merely manipulable objects to being classifiable and knowable by other objects.

In other words, in the age-old debate between Anaxagoras (who claimed that humans are the most intelligent animals because they have hands) and Aristotle (who argued that humans have hands precisely because of their superior intelligence), I unequivocally side with the former. The "cognitive revolution" that supposedly occurred around seventy thousand years ago depended on our increasing systematic use of technology. It did not happen the other way around, with our cognitive abilities improving and subsequently leading to a more systematic use of technology. Cognition, like any natural element, evolves gradually, whereas technology progresses rapidly within the cultural revolution because it capitalizes on the past. When a system of technological apparatuses reaches a critical mass, it becomes the catalyst for the cognitive revolution.

3.4 Culture as Second Nature

Behold, the techno-anthropological circle: on one hand, what we are stems from technology; on the other hand, the will to live of automata finds new life and new horizons precisely through humans. For it is the technical supplements that, by determining our form of life, will determine the specifics of natural human intelligence, setting it apart from other organisms. We do not *learn* how to live but *get used to living* thanks to our second nature that retroactively impacts the first. The transition from nature to second nature, from lived life to examined life, not only characterizes the human animal but is also the quintessence of that exclusively human process known as education. In fact, the teachings a cat imparts to its kittens or the flight lessons a magpie provides are not education but training because they reach an upper threshold very quickly and do not possess the infinite developmental nature intrinsic to the education of our species.

Consider the difference between reading a novel or a historical treatise and reading instructions for a water heater. Once we have absorbed the instructions, there is nothing more to be done except apply what we have learned, placing us in a similar position to cats or magpies. However, we have something that appears exclusively human. The act of reading a treatise or a novel extends beyond a singular application and beckons the exploration of additional treatises and novels. This process, often labeled as 'infinite,' is more accurately described as indefinite, for nowhere is it written that, once we've finished reading a book, there is no reason to read another. Nonetheless, there will undeniably come a day when we will stop reading altogether, as mortality claims us.

4. From Human Capital to Human Heritage

When recorded, the techno-anthropological circle transforms human capital into an asset of humanity. At present, we are witnessing a vast and inequitable production of surplus value in which humanity as a whole—including retirees, children, the unemployed, and the otherwise occupied—generates value that is enjoyed solely by a select few platforms. Already at this level, consumption, the quintessential form of human life, is undergoing a profound transformation. From its previous state of wastefulness, it is evolving into the most remarkable generator of value that humanity has ever witnessed. While production, driven by merit, is subject to increasing automation, consumption, born from consumption itself, emerges as the primary wellspring of all value, both in conceptual and economic terms. The task at hand is to ensure the equitable redistribution of this capital—the documedial surplus value—for the greater benefit and well-being of humanity as a whole.

This heritage is first of all *new*, for although the consumption acts it records date back to the origins of the human species, they have not been, until now, documented and transformed into data, into potential capital. Moreover, this new heritage is *rich*, as it does not merely document wealth or possessions, but rather captures the thoughts, words, deeds, likes and dislikes of humans who continually enrich the vast archive from which artificial intelligence draws its wisdom. Thirdly, this heritage is *renewable*, since data ownership has the public character of ideas: unlike tangible assets, data can be shared without loss. Finally, and above all, it is an *equitable* heritage, emerging not from the inherently contentious and subjective concept of merit, but rather from the inexhaustible and egalitarian force of need that makes all humans equal.

4.1 A New Heritage

The human heritage is ontologically new. Acts that have characterized the human way of life (walking, watching, consuming, appreciating, fearing) for millions of years, and that have left no or very few traces so far and only in solemn circumstances, are now being recorded and transformed into documents. This represents a qualitative and quantitative change: the anthropic mass has reached unprecedented heights, a circumstance that potentially turns into a possible resource what is effectively the root cause of the environmental crisis. All these forms of life are being meticulously recorded, a departure from the past where traces were elusive. These are acts that we rarely consciously acknowledge. Who keeps track of the precise time and location when they searched for a restaurant? We may cough multiple times during a phone call without paying much attention to it, and when asked how many times, we would struggle to recall. Similarly, there are actions we know we perform but refrain from quantifying, for how many of us, before the advent of the smart phone, counted their steps during a walk? Many experiences that would have gone unnoticed without the Web, like monitoring our biorhythms, now find their place in recorded history. It is far more important to recognize this capital than to discover a new world or conquer space, for it signifies the proliferation of objects and meanings within our own world.

The critical and decisive realm where humanity's heritage is produced is what I have called the "docusphere," a vast repository of human life forms that introduce into the world an infinite variety of objects that previously left no trace. The fact that the computer to which I am currently dictating or on which I am typing keeps track of the time and location of my input does not require any deliberate intention on my part. This seamless operation is cost-effective and encompasses a wealth of data, ranging from my geolocation and body temperature to the direc-

tion of my gaze, capturing everything I did before and after this dictation. These unassuming yet significant aspects herald a Copernican revolution that now more than ever underscores the indispensability of theory.

**The new resources, in fact, would be incomprehensible from a
theoretical standpoint if we were to adopt the mainstream perspective
that treats social reality as a mere reflection of the actions and thoughts
of its actors, an approach I refer to as** *intentionalism.* Intentionalism, by
tying social reality to collective intentionality, deprives social objects of
their autonomous ontological reality, reducing them to mere reflections
of mental operations. The most influential exponent of intentionalism,
the U.S. philosopher John Searle, has spoken of an "immense invisible
ontology" consisting of social objects.[1] However, he did not specify
whether these objects were novel, and this ambiguity is understandable
since he had in mind an ontology subordinate to physical entities and
collective psychology. Searle's reliance on the constitutive rule that X
counts as Y in C for social objects, positions them as composites of
physical entities (natural or artificial) on one hand and collective intentionality on the other. The subsequent definition of social objects as
mere outcomes of collective intentionality[2] undermines their autonomy
in relation to the intentional states that produce them. In philosophical
terms, intentionalism reveals itself as the direct heir to transcendental
idealism, wherein the self constructs its own world, which, therefore, is
but a reflection of its creator's thoughts and will.

Just as transcendental idealism dissolved into a nihilism in general
ontology, intentionalism gives rise to a nihilism in social ontology, with
political implications that prevent us from relying on the collective human heritage to address the challenges posed by automation. Moreover,
from a theoretical standpoint, intentionalism fails to provide a satisfac-
tory response to the question of why platform services are frequently offered free of charge. Why indeed? If there were no financial interest, the

1   John R. Searle, *The Construction of Social Reality* (New York: Free Press, 1995).
2   John R. Searle, *Making the Social World: The Structure of Human Civilization* (Ox-
     ford and New York: Oxford University Press, 2010).

behavior of platforms would be inexplicable. But if we view data as the mere shadow of collective intentionality, then we will equally fail to understand why platforms go to so much trouble to collect it, and above all, we won't be able to understand how it is possible to collect something that does not exist. **To account for the existence and autonomy of data, a realistic perspective rooted in social ontology is required. This perspective embraces the thesis of** *documentalism,* which contends that social objects are much more than mere reflections of the intentions of social actors, just as the artworks showcased in a gallery are more than mere reminders of the artists' ideas.

Within this framework, the Web emerges as an enormous social objects machine giving rise to a comprehensive archive of human life where everything is written. It encompasses both intentional communication (even an audio message is writing, because it is repeatable) but also the vast expanse of data documenting our actions, even those we never consciously intend to produce. **From the perspective of documentalism, the constitutive rule of social objects—including data—can be stated as Object = Recorded Act. These social objects (data) emerge as the result of recorded social acts, embodying the intricacies of human behavior and meticulously preserved in some form of medium.**[3] The result is none other than the docusphere, a vast territory that would disappear without the act of recording. Yet, when documented, it gives rise to a tangible digital heritage that transcends the realm of the virtual, as it keeps track not of thoughts and intentions but of actions. By emphasizing the constitutive ontological nature of recording, which emancipates the object from the producing subject, documentalism goes beyond the perception of social objects as mere reflections of intentionality and recognizes intentionality itself as a reflection and derivative of social objects. This not only explains how data (unlike collective intentionality and other phantom entities) can be capitalized, but also why individual intentionality—what we are and what we want—is significantly shaped by the surrounding environment, primarily a documentary context. Social intentions and desires, everything that goes beyond the immediate satisfac-

---

3   Ferraris, *Documentality,* cit.

tion of organic needs, emerge from the encounter of a living body that supplies vitality and need with a documentary structure that determines the form that intentionality takes, namely the orientation of our higher and culturally determined needs.

Now, the following consideration arises: To assert that nothing exists outside the text[4] is an ontologically false and epistemologically unoriginal statement, as it merely suggests that intuitions devoid of concepts are blind and that conceptual frameworks play a constitutive role in knowledge acquisition. However, it becomes an ontologically valid and epistemologically groundbreaking assertion when we recognize that *nothing social exists outside the text*. Here, the "text" refers to the power of record keeping and capitalization that predates the so-called "civilizations of writing," as exemplified by the pivotal role of capitalization in human civilization and confirmed by the explosion of recording on the Web. Finally, it can become an economically and politically intriguing proposition when we transform the necessary condition (nothing social exists outside the text) into a sufficient condition (if there is a text, then there is something social). By demonstrating how recording has the power to bring forth objects that otherwise would not exist, we can establish that what is produced through the documentation of human forms of life is an entirely novel and ever-growing capital.

In the pre-digital era, when every human action was not automatically recorded, consumption left little to no traces. However, today, consumption and the intricate web of human activity surrounding it for various purposes (needs, desires, useful or futile acts, curiosity, and multifaceted necessities in an animal structurally inclined towards dependence). It is produces value, i.e., data capital. It is this very data that progressively makes humans as producers more and more obsolete. Yet, it is precisely this data that also works a miracle that no revolution had ever performed: humans are no longer valued solely for their physical prowess, patience, or precision, nor are they merely regarded as incidental parts of a machine. Rather, they become indispensable because of

---

4   Jacques Derrida, *Of Grammatology* (Baltimore and London: The Johns Hopkins University Press, 1976).

their being human, as bearers of preferences, interests, and values, i.e., of a diverse array of needs and consumptions that give machines sight and substance.

4.2 A Rich Heritage

This human heritage is *epistemologically rich*. Unlike banking capital, which informs us about the assets of others, or financial capital, which reflects human expectations about the future, the human heritage provides us with a detailed, varied, and unprecedented panorama of human life forms. This heritage, if appropriately interpreted, possesses the potential to furnish us with a social physics as robust as natural physics. We find ourselves amidst an epistemological revolution whose magnitude we have yet to fully grasp. The traditional dichotomy between nature as the realm of necessity and society as the realm of liberty is now inverted: the more we deepen our knowledge of nature, the more it reveals chaotic and unpredictable phenomena; whereas the more we grow in our understanding of human behavior through data generated by our actions, the more these behaviors appear predictable and uniform.

First and foremost, there is an advantage in terms of **analysis**. In the analog world, recording data and making it replicable requires careful deliberation, attention, and energy. Not so in the digital world, where the only energy required is the electricity that powers the machines. Moreover, in the analog world simply consulting and comparing data requires expertise, skill, patience, and time that, in the case of large textual corpora, can exceed the lifetime of a human being. These recording and consultation limits do not apply to the world of data, leading to a change of scale. Anyone walking into a restaurant at eight o'clock in the evening would be able to predict that in four hours, the place will be empty (unless it is New Year's Eve). The scope of predictability has now expanded exponentially, underscoring the potential value of this new capital. Companies like Amazon engage in profiling individual behaviors not for policing purposes but rather to leverage the knowledge of individual consumption patterns. This allows the company to send unsolicited goods to customers (only 3% refuse the merchandise), as they respond to the personalized preferences of the profiled individuals with surgical precision.

The encounter between machines and humans generates a powerful form of **prediction**. Machines have become increasingly proficient at replicating the past, enabling precise projections for the future, as nature, whether organic or spiritual, tends to repeat itself more often than we might think. However, what no machine can do, primarily because it has never faced the urgency of metabolism, is to project itself into the future or devise ways to meet future needs—a necessity inconceivable for any mechanism while inevitable for every organism. The mouse approaching the cheese is aware of the future while the trap about to snap does not have the faintest idea. In the case of humans, desire and trap, organism and mechanism, are inherently entwined. Consequently, humans can be perfected and educated—processes that will be further explored in the next chapter.

The abundance of data also fuels **invention**, a natural outcome of the exponential growth of the archive. The Neapolitan philosopher Giambattista Vico astutely observed that the archive of the moderns dwarfs its ancient counterpart. This means that we have a far greater quantity of models and examples. This is all the more true today as the explosion of documents in the age of recording has created an archive that has no equivalent in history. This, too, is an advantage that we do not sufficiently reflect upon, and that should serve as a foundation of a fourth *New Science*, following Vico's three—a collective endeavor in times like ours that, contrary to prevailing belief, are exceptionally favorable to humanism. "Invention" is both the act of invention and that which is invented, encompassing not only concrete manifestations but also abstract ideations, the conception of something completely new. However, it is worth remembering that in legal and ecclesiastical language, both more attuned to the etymology of *inventio*, it also refers to the discovery of a treasure or relic, that is, of something that was previously hidden, subsequently found, and then inventoried. In this sense, *inventio* aligns with the rhetorical quest for arguments and the scholastic process of discovering (or, often, rediscovering) ideas. This arsenal and armory of arguments and ideas has reached its apex in the age of documedia capital.

4.3 A Renewable Heritage

Thirdly, this human heritage is **renewable** in several ways. When I, as a data producer in a digital economy request to retrieve my data from a platform, I do not harm the platform's economy since I do not deprive it of its resources. Instead, I gain possession of a good that, when combined with that of others within a humanistic or mutualistic platform, will allow me to create value to be redistributed with humanistic motivations. This realization addresses the ethical concerns of philosophers and all well-intentioned individuals while simultaneously increasing economic resources.

Embedded within this consideration lies a crucial element of data, namely its **shareability**. By virtue of being recorded and therefore iterable, data takes on a level of abstraction resembling ideas rather than things. If I give someone a barrel of oil, I lose possession of it, but if I give away billions of data, I still retain ownership, although not exclusively. This might not necessarily be a disadvantage, as it is possible that the alternative use of my data could still benefit me. If that were not the case, if syntactic capital were a commodity like oil or steel, it would be difficult to ask platforms to share it. Indeed, platforms could argue that without their investment, foresight, and research, it would not have been possible to transform the forms of human life into wealth. But as we just saw, unlike oil and steel, you get to share your data and keep it. In this sense, data sharing bears no resemblance to expropriation.

Linked to iterability is that fact that, in addition to being sharable, data is **recyclable. This means that it can be used over an indefinite period** albeit in this case, too, the consumption of non-renewable resources such as electricity is necessary for data to be iterated. Shareability and recyclability form the bedrock of the potential for alternative capitalization, a core principle underpinning the Web. Instead of advocating for the Web's status as a common good or lamenting the capitalization of commercial platforms, it is necessary to mobilize intermediary bodies such as associations, institutions, mutual societies, and unions that seem to have lost their traditional roles but have the potential to find new purpose through the capitalization of the human forms of life.

An additional aspect stemming from iterability is the possibility of **semantic recontextualization:** syntactic data can become semantic (acquire meaning), depending on how it is processed. This process bears resemblance to the distinction between, but also permutability of, 'strong' documents (registration of deeds) and 'weak' documents (recording of facts), which I explored elsewhere.[5] Consider, for instance, a testament and a separate inventory of assets prepared by the testator. These represent two distinct practices: the former is a deed that disposes of something, while the latter is a memorandum or a record that simply provides an account of existing items. This difference forms the basis for differentiating between a strong document, which is performative and determines the existence of a social object, and a weak document, which is merely the record of a fact, although its function can have epistemological implications. For a future historian, the difference between the will and the inventory may appear irrelevant if their purpose is to ascertain the testator's assets. But there is no doubt that these two texts are fundamentally different in nature.

These characteristics can be summarized by the fact that the fundamental nature of the goods that comprise the human heritage is **intangibility**. It is necessary to avoid the naturalistic fallacy according to which data is raw material. From this perspective, the metaphor of data as the new oil is misleading for a number of reasons related to the difference between tangible and intangible goods. We said that, unlike oil, data is renewable; it is not a physical commodity but rather a recording of life forms; being digital, it does not require the same levels of resource-intensive extraction processes, refinement, and distribution; finally, it does not generate energy but requires it. The latter circumstance, however, poses a limit to renewability. Renewability applies to data but not to its production and management. Intangibility, thus, does not preclude a

---

5   Ferraris, *Documentality*, cit.

link to **materiality**, which does not concern the content of the data, but the supports that enable its extraction, storge, and circulation.

While the digital realm was once heralded as immaterial,[6] today we recognize that 2% of greenhouse gas emissions (equivalent to those generated by air travel) are associated with data management,[7] particularly the proliferation of Blockchain technology.[8] Additionally, the raw materials required for digital technology pose two significant challenges: On one hand, no European nation is a primary producer of metals and rare earth while China appears both in a favorable position in terms of resources and imperiled by the environmental repercussions of extraction activities. Of course, a judicious use of these technologies could reduce greenhouse gas emissions by 20% by 2023.[9] It is within this context that academia, industry, and politics must forge alliances following the core tenets of the Webfare project.

4.4 An Equitable Heritage

With human heritage, a general economy is delineated, which confers economic value to what was traditionally considered worthless or wasteful. In this deep reevaluation lies the foundation for a democracy of needs that fuels Webfare. Indeed, this heritage makes no distinctions between rich and poor, beautiful or ugly, intelligent or foolish. For even those without a penny to their name, burdened by misfortune, and deemed unsightly, wicked, or dim-witted, provided that they have internet access, generate a data heritage that is equal to and more important than the heritage produced by the richest, most beautiful, and smartest

---

6   Jean-François Lyotard, "Les immatériaux," *Art & Text*, 1985.

7   Luciano Floridi, *Il verde e il blu: Idee ingenue per migliorare la politica* (Milano: Cortina, 2022).

8   Ellen Meijer, "Blockchain and Our Planet: Why Such High Energy Use?" *Pre-Sustainability*, June 6, 2022, https://pre-sustainability.com/articles/blockchain-and-our-planet-why-such-high-energy-use/

9   Global e-Sustainability Initiative GeSI, https://gesi.org/research/gesi-smarter-2020-the-role-of-ict-in-driving-a-sustainable-future

humans on earth. This because such a heritage is more representative of the collective, average human experience. We are thus breaking free from the shackles of past capitalization models, intricately tied to the exploitation of the many and the presumed merits of the few. Neither do we embrace a totalitarian instrument of control or indulge in the perilous utopia of a world fueled by the rarest and most unreliable of human endowments: intelligence. The crucial political dimension of humanity's heritage resides in emphasizing the significance of need in the formation of value, in contrast to the emphasis on ability that characterized capitalization in pre-automated production.

It has rightly been observed that need, and its amplified form, desire, are revolutionary.[10] Indeed, on behalf of what are revolutions waged if not to satisfy needs and desires? It has also been noted that desire is a fundamental element of economy,[11] and indeed there would be no economy without needs to fulfill. **The novelty here is that need emerges as a factor of capitalization, assuming a paramount role in the entire process. While the ancient Greeks emphasized that in the beginning was the logos, and modern humans wrote that in the beginning there was action, the humans of today and of the future must recognize that in the beginning, and even more so in the end, there is passion, manifested through need, as the essential catalyst for the origin, growth, and ultimate meaning of capitalization.**

What does it mean to be human? Does it mean to think? To create? No, it means to consume, to manifest needs in a techno-socio-economic system. Precisely because, unlike machines, we are destined for a radical interruption, it is we who through consumption imbue the entire process with purpose, direction, and value. Hence, we witness the emergence of a general economy, seamlessly integrating consumption, thereby transforming it into value and, above all, knowledge. **Within**

---

10   Gilles Deleuze and Félix Guattari, *Anti-Oedipus: Capitalism and Schizophrenia* (New York: Viking Press, 1972); Ágnes Heller, *Towards a Marxist Theory of Value* (Carbondale, IL: Southern Illinois University, 1972).

11   Jean-François Lyotard, *Libidinal Economy* (Bloomington, IN: Indiana University Press, 1974).

this all-encompassing paradigm, the human heritage is *teleologically, that is, ethically, equitable.* Instead of a sign of divine favoritism for an individual, as in the Calvinist genesis of bourgeois capital, this Catholic capital—in the etymological sense of Catholicism as "universality"—grows in value when shared among all human beings, regardless of wealth, intelligence, ethnicity, or faith. **Cooperation reigns supreme and the concept of the free rider fades into insignificance.** Without appealing to (an often disregarded) ethics, data in itself fosters a sense of solidarity that counteracts individual selfishness. Its very essence and interpretation demonstrate that humans can truly only benefit from aggregated data, i.e., from a cooperative attitude, while individual data holds little value in itself. This results in a system of valorization that does not privilege the individual and labor, but rather collectivity and need, which some may view as a potentially repressive desublimation, unaware of the vast and novel possibilities that it offers.

From here, a whole new purpose for philosophical and social reflection emerges: to **outline a capitalization system driven by humanistic platforms that offer an alternative, non-competitive approach to liberalist platforms,** which, for their part, have successfully harnessed a new source of value. If the revolutionary drive comes from capital, then true revolutionaries do not wage war against it; instead, they envision alternative capitalization processes. In this sense, the pursuit of "the greatest happiness for the greatest number of people" becomes a questionable moral project. Because not only would it be problematic to base humanity's happiness on the happiness of a single individual, but, as ample evidence suggests, happiness itself is hard to define and is rarely the primary goal of humans. It is much more reasonable to focus not on delivering happiness but on providing resources: "from each according to their abilities, to each according to their needs." After all, we cannot guarantee universal happiness unless we resort to something as whimsical as laughing gas. However, as moral beings, we can and should ensure that humanity is not overburdened by needs, enabling humans to pursue growth, education, and progress.

This would allow humanity to achieve a level of dignity indispensable for life to be genuinely worth living. However, the point is that the society that emerged with the birth of agriculture over the past ten thousand years places more emphasis on merit (as seen through the lens of labor) rather than need. **It is thus not at all difficult to reward merit; indeed, this is common practice, with the result that a tiny fraction of humans have superior resources to billions of their peers.** This is a form of ideological representation in which merit becomes the ultimate reference for inequality even if it may have nothing to do with merit itself.

The conceptualization of a human heritage brings about what has long appeared merely a chimera—the recognition of need on par with merit.[12] This forms the crux of justice as access to substantive rather than just formal rights. This is also the reason why, until now, fulfilling this aspiration has proved elusive. Strictly speaking it is right that everyone is given what they deserve according to their abilities and contribution to society. To receive something based on one's needs is far more difficult to justify not only because needs traditionally involve asking rather than giving. But mainly because it is difficult to determine the precise measure of an individual's needs, distinguish them from desires, and perhaps even from excesses.

Nevertheless, as we saw, human life generates and is the ultimate foundation of value. This means that all humans connected through the Web create value, but only those without other means of income could potentially receive dividends from capitalization. If we could harness and redistribute to all of humanity the value derived from the capitalization of needs—a capital whose most conspicuous manifestation today is the Web—we would take a decisive step towards the attainment of

---

12   Karl Marx, *Critique of the Gotha Programme*, in Marx and Engels, *Selected Works*, Vol. 3 (Moscow: Progress Publishers, 1970, pp.13–30: "In a higher phase of communist society, after the enslaving subordination of the individual to the division of labor, and therewith also the antithesis between mental and physical labor, has vanished; after labor has become not only a means of life but life's prime want; after the productive forces have also increased with the all-around development of the individual, and all the springs of co-operative wealth flow more abundantly – only then can the narrow horizon of bourgeois right be crossed in its entirety and society inscribe on its banners: From each according to his ability, to each according to his needs!"

the highest good. **One may wonder whether this valorization of need only serves a moral imperative. This is not the case. A sound economic rationale underpins this proposition. In an era of automated production, it is essential to recognize that what is required above all is need precisely because it cannot be automated and is therefore a primary source of value.**

Ultimately, human needs define the value of things. Whether immediate, like hunger or thirst, or more abstract, like emotional, social, or cultural interests, our needs have always determined the value of goods. This principle becomes particularly important as technology increasingly supplants human involvement in the production of goods. No longer involved in the production of goods, humans become producers of value, viz., they determine the essence, necessity, and thus value of production based on their unique peculiarities and preferences in the act of consumption recorded by the Web.

5. From Homo Faber to Homo Sapiens

The last century has brought a surprising turn of events. **A hundred years ago many believed that we would witness the end of capitalism and the triumph of labor. However, the opposite has proven true:** work is slowly but steadily disappearing because of automation while, alongside industrial and financial capital, a new form of capital has emerged—documedia capital. If the considerations made so far hold even a modicum of credibility, this new capital could transform into a human heritage that addresses the demands of social justice far more effectively than the notion of the end of capital and the triumph of labor. Before we delve into the concrete proposal of Webfare, we must contemplate what will take the place of labor in defining human nature.

5.1 Relativization

I use **"labor" and "work" interchangeably and define them as any act of an organism, usually a human, capable of producing potential value by interacting with technical apparatuses** such as oars, plows, pens, or computer keyboards. Thus, a natural function such as walking becomes work when it involves pulling a cart, thereby producing value (if the cart is a rickshaw, for instance). Conversely, any value production transforms an interaction between organisms and mechanisms into labor as is the case, for instance, when a smartwatch records my biometrics while I sleep. However, while for the time being it might not seem prudent to abandon the concept of "labor" altogether, it should be immediately pointed out that what platforms capitalize on is seldom underpaid labor but non-coercive mobilization. Labor is the production of value, which **suggests that the production of goods—the activity of *homo faber*—is but one moment in the relationship of humans to labor or, conversely, that labor is just one epoch of human history**. It is indeed a conceptual error to claim—as is often done—that *we* are the product, since we do not live in a slave economy. But it is not an error to claim that we are *producers*, namely, that we work, often for free, and financing out of our own pockets the means of production while producing documents in collaboration with the Web, much like the textile workers in Manchester during the time of Marx produced cloth in cooperation with looms.

It is true that we might not know how to use those documents and that they wouldn't even be collected without the major internet companies. But it is also true that, without us, the documents would not exist. This situation reproduces the classic relationship between capital and labor, with a very important variation, namely that this labor is not remunerated, and indeed, not even recognized as such. **It is therefore necessary to relativize the status of labor as an alleged absolute of humanity.** Even the tombs of the Cro-Magnon contained jewelry and hinted at differences in status. However, ever since the emergence of agriculture in the 'fertile crescent,' humanity has differentiated between the privileged who benefit from good education and intergenerational inheritance of wealth, and the dispossessed and potentially damned of the earth.

Over time, certain mechanisms were abandoned that were meant to bridge social disparities as in the case of debt forgiveness when a new ruler would ascend the throne in Mesopotamia. This because debt relationships were no longer incurred between the ruler and the subjects but among equal citizens. From that moment on, the difference between those born into wealth and the dispossessed became a constant in the social world, often justified by attributing such differences to natural factors such as caste, race, gender, or divine providence. None of us find this fair. In principle, we reject it, although we all experience moments of superiority or subalternity in our lives. Yet we are not genuinely astonished by the fact that there are the rich and the poor, whether in the Global South or in our backyard. If we accept in fact what we reject in law, it is because the law has yet to rectify the fact. **It is worth noting that the society of** *homo faber* **for most of its history conferred merits regardless of labor**. In traditional societies, being noble, a priest, or a soldier used to entail merit independent of labor, and this still holds true to some extent for religious figures and military personnel. Let us not forget that until half a century ago, it was considered normal for half of humanity—women—not to work in a formally recognized way but to dedicate themselves to family care.

5.2 Rarefaction

The picture that emerges is truly paradoxical: the twentieth century as the century of labor, identifying formal engagement in production or service as constitutive of the identity of every adult human being, is also the century that ends with the prophecy of the end of labor. A prophecy that, for once, is coming true, although it does not take much to predict that plumbers will still be around for decades, and that professional athletes, generals, priests, psychoanalysts, and porn stars will probably continue to work in an almost entirely automated society. Our task, therefore, is to sketch the evolving forms of humanity in the era of the rarefaction of *homo faber*.

Let us start with an obvious fact: Production and distribution will increasingly be handled by robots, machines designed for work (*работа*). And as data is efficiently used to automate work processes, it is the workers who will disappear. If one were to observe contemporary society with an outsider's perspective, they might feel as if they were witnessing a world of hunters and gatherers, bustling and moving, perhaps even toiling, but mostly engaged in contemplating and manipulating small objects that they never put down. **Rather than a disappearance of** *homo faber*, **we are witnessing his rarefaction**. A reimagining of the Benedictine rule *ora et labora* may soon sideline the labor: codex copying has been an automated activity for centuries, and agricultural workers in Italy who only a century ago comprised half of the nation's workforce, now make up only 2%. During the age of geographical discoveries, Europeans who came into contact with the inhabitants of Santo Domingo or New Caledonia, that is, with hunter-gatherers, described them as idle people merely taking advantage of nature's bounty. If one of our ancestors from the early twentieth century were to come back from the dead, they would describe us as even lazier than the Caribs or Canachi. Instead of sweating in fields and workshops, we sit in bars or on trains, merely fiddling with our cell phones, and we only break a sweat to burn calories while running for sport.

Let us delve deeper into the characteristics of this rarefaction, which is, of course, also a transformation. Automation and digitalization have reduced the number of medium-paying jobs and widened the gap between high-paying and low-paying jobs, as what is done at the two extremes cannot be automated. Considering this situation, one might be tempted to say that few things seem as certain as these two axioms: the future of work lies in technical-scientific specialization, and the middle class, if it not on the brink of extinction, will soon disappear. Now, both axioms are false. As we read in the report *Il Futuro delle Competenze in Italia* (*The Future of Skills in Italy*), the result of research conducted by Ernst and Young, Pearson Italia, and ManpowerGroup, the jobs of the future will largely involve an eclectic hybridization of skills with a strong humanistic component. By 2030, the middle class will increase by 2 billion, reaching 5.3 billion, representing 61.6% of the world's population estimated at 8.6 billion. The spontaneous question arises of how we will live, how we will survive, if in the meantime (according to the report) 43.50% (345 professions) are in decline, 20.30% (161 professions) are stable, and only 36.20% (287 professions) are predicted to grow. Strictly speaking, rather than witnessing the growth of the middle class, we could be facing universal poverty.

When humans were seen as imperfect appendages to scythes, hammers, typewriters, and bureaucratic counters, manpower was an important commodity; now, this is no longer the case, and those occupations are often paid much less. It is also true that among the new jobs there are some that involve relatively simple tasks such as pizza home delivery that are not yet within the capabilities of machines but that give the impression of a future of work not much different from the industrial past, albeit with fewer rights. It is unlikely, however, that it will end this way, and those tasks will eventually be performed by drones and artificial intelligence following investments in research and development based on a simple and decisive argument: machines, which neither die nor have rights, are more cost-effective than any human. This opens an even more troubling dystopia—that of a world of outcasts where machines have entirely replaced humans, perhaps even in consumption. But to say this is to misunderstand the nature of automation.

Let us take a moment to reflect. Automation is the response to human needs and needs cannot be automated; therefore, the more automation advances, the more machines become dependent on humans. A stick is a useful tool even for a chimpanzee, but it would not know what to do with a cell phone. From this simple insight, we can understand the nature of the jobs of the future. In an influential 2013 article examining the impact of computerization on work, Carl Benedikt Frey and Michael A. Osborne[1] analyzed 702 occupations and found an advantage in creative and specialized jobs. In essence, this is predictable: the invention of photography was supposed to make painters disappear; instead, in the medium term, it is photographers who disappeared. But there is much more in the case of *Il futuro delle competenze in Italia*.[2] The most valuable assets of the future are primarily relational and new jobs emerge from this humanistic-technological foundation, on the basis of three processes: The first process involves the creation of jobs that did not previously exist and that require a mix of psychological and technological skills for the design, for instance, of the interfaces of self-driving cars or virtual assistants. The second process concerns the destruction of old jobs to make way for new ones: the various specializations of several

1   Carl Benedikt Frey and Michael A. Osborne, "The Future of Employment: How Susceptible Are Jobs to Computerisation?" Working paper published by the Oxford Martin Programme on the Impact of Future Technology, September 1, 2013, https://www.oxfordmartin.ox.ac.uk/publications/the-future-of-emplo yment/

2   At the international level, see the data collected by the OECD, "Data on the Future of Work," https://www.oecd.org/future-of-work/reports-and-data/data -infographics.htm, last accessed July 26, 2023.

workers are merged into a single position that entails the integration and coordination of assembly robots. The third is a process of mutation, where a profession develops by adopting characteristics from other professions (we can be sure that without computer science we would not discover vaccines as quickly).

Describing these new jobs requires lengthy periphrases because they are all the result of hybridization, a process of merging skills that will affect many traditional jobs, and not only journalists or corporate lawyers, but manual workers and maintenance staff too. Only a human can tell whether a stretch of highway needs repair, even though, in performing the task, they will merely control machines and check their results. According to the report, dentists (one of the oldest professions in the world), notaries, lawyers, architects, and psychologists are immune to hybridization. However, their way of working has changed: dentists use 3D scanning technologies, and it is precisely this use of technology that makes a profession hybrid. The impact on architecture is similarly enormous.[3] Yet one thing is clear: while a few years ago, no one could have imagined that designing interfaces could be a job and being a typist would cease to be one, as technology evolves, humans will still have toothaches, depressions, arguments, as well as the need for homes and mortgages to buy them.

One problem remains though, namely, that those with a low-level education and obsolete training will struggle to fit into this new world of hybridization of complex technological and humanistic skills. But even in those cases, being human and not a machine will protect them from being replaced, not only because humans possess the understanding and empathy that machines lack (instead of acting like delivery drones, they could advantageously replace the hideous companion robots that are currently being designed); but also because all humans possess something irreplaceable and uniquely human: the organic need for consumption and the value of production that it generates through

---

3   Mario Carpo, *The Second Digital Turn: Design Beyond Intelligence* (Cambridge, MA: The MIT Press, 2017) and *Beyond Digital: Design and Automation at the End of Modernity* (Cambridge, MA: The MIT Press, 2023).

their mobilization on the Web—a priceless and irreplaceable value, if we know how to recognize it, at a time when humans have stopped imitating machines and machines just cannot stop imitating humans.

5.3 Mobilization

There is a further aspect worth considering. A rudimentary technology such as chipping flint to make a scraper marked the beginning of humanity by turning humans into appendages of machines. This applies to the combination of human, plow, and oxen too, where physical strength, patience, discipline, self-forgetfulness, and alienation were demanded just as in the human-hammer-anvil feedback system or the assembly line, where humans perform tasks easily replaceable by automatons. A more advanced technique involves using humans for regulation purposes only in theory. In practice, the transformation of workers into machine controllers and then into intellectuals emancipated from the grips of capital has not taken place. This because automation has also extended to the intellectual functions of the supervisors, i.e., to the regulators and controllers themselves. The idea of workers as controllers, plausible at the time when Marx wrote what is known today as "The Fragment on Machines," is now problematic because machine learning aims to replace humans in any control task. If anything, humans are necessary precisely in such tasks where it is not their higher cognitive abilities that count but merely the ability to perform a simple task (such as recognition). Why? Because these are easy for organisms but extremely complicated for mechanisms.

Considering the direction that technology is taking, let us restate again what has been said thus far: **There is one function where humans as organisms can never be replaced, namely need and the resulting consumption as the *exclusive* characteristic of the living.** To fully grasp this is to arrive at a revolutionary conclusion because, in the world of classical production, physical effort and human endeavor (i.e., merit) always prevailed. However, when production is automated or automatable, consumption becomes the most precious asset, the goal without which the production process would be meaningless. **Less and less mere cogs in a machine, but now and always the origin and goal of mechanisms, we mobilize, that is, we practice our normal forms of life that, when recorded on the Web, produce data, i.e., value.**

Mobilization is the condition in which humans in developed countries find themselves. As the demand for laborious and alienating work decreases, humanity does not become passive, as in the dystopian vision of a world vegetating in front of a screen. Rather, we become producers of documents. We are mobilized when we spend time on the web and are therefore productive not for ourselves but for others. Whether we occupy our time with writing nonsense, overeat, idle around, or torment others, we are never bored because we always have a smartphone or a similar device in our hands. The point is not the value of what we do but the value that can be derived from the interpretation and capitalization of the data we produce. Can we call "labor" a mobilization that can also occur *sur place*? For the moment, since we are in the middle of the ford, the answer is affirmative.

With the concept of "mobilization," I hope to have provided some answers to many pressing questions. What happens with work when *homo faber* is gradually left in the tool shed? Moreover, does it become something else or simply disappear? It is too early to say. Globally, *homo faber* is still the most widespread species in the human fauna, but, as we have seen, in our parts he is becoming rarified. Some traditional jobs will survive, as new ones will likely emerge, but not as many as those that will have disappeared, nor will they be as appealing.[4] Others may be paid much less than they used to because reduced demand. However, it is highly probable that automation will render a significant portion of our current jobs unnecessary, just as it happened with agricultural jobs, which, let us not forget, a century ago employed the

---

4   Darrell M. West, "What Happens if Robots Take the Jobs? The Impact of Emerging Technologies on Employment and Public Policy," *Brookings*, October 26, 2015, https://www.brookings.edu/articles/what-happens-if-robots-take-the-jobs-the-impact-of-emerging-technologies-on-employment-and-public-policy/

majority of the human population. Indeed, many sections of society are negatively affected by the ongoing transformation[5] and by the devaluation of traditional jobs.[6] So much so that, the concept of work in the future—assuming and not conceding that there will be work,[7] which, all things considered, is still preferable to the more widespread prophecy of a jobless future—cannot be confined to the traditional modern wage labor, primarily because that type of work is becoming increasingly rare. One point, however, should not be forgotten: there is nothing noble or beautiful in toil. In the context of their literary endeavors, it remains an undeniable truth that neither Gabriele D'Annunzio, with his notion of *bella fatica* ("beautiful labor"), nor Giacomo Leopardi, with his *sudate carte* ("sweat-soaked pages"), would have been willing to toil and sweat in any other way than with the pen.

Those who advocate a return to the factories do not speak for themselves but for others, simply checking the empty box of the human identified with the industrial worker. This explains the stigma that today affects the so-called "shit jobs," positions somehow considered one level above "bullshit jobs,"[8] as if taking dictation for eight hours for a modest salary (also known as a typist) were not a garbage job from our contemporary perspective, or as if the blessed days of the assembly line or galley rowing were not far worse than garbage jobs. There is also nothing beautiful in dreaming of an idyllic primitivism.[9]

5   Luis Garicano and Esteban Rossi-Hansberg, "Organization and Inequality in a Knowledge Economy," *The Quarterly Journal of Economics*, 121:4 (2016): 1383–1435.

6   Laura Abrandi, Carlo Cambini, and Laura Rondi, "Artificial Intelligence, Firms and Consumer Behavior: A Survey," *Journal of Economic Surveys* 36 (2022): 969–991.

7   Daniel Susskind, *A World Without Work: Technology, Automation, and How We Should Respond* (London: Allen Lane, 2020).

8   David Graeber, *Bullshit Jobs. A Theory* (New York: Simon & Schuster, 2018).

9   James Suzman, *Work: A History of How We Spend Our Time* (London: Bloomsbury, 2020).

5.4 Valorization

"Consumers of the world, unite!" Considering what has been said so far, this is neither an ironic nor a paradoxical message. Rather, it is a realistic and essential slogan at a time when workers are disappearing, and their union would only result in negative capital and a great financial liability. In contrast, the union of consumers generates the human heritage. Even those who, traditionally, had to start out with nothing but their own bodies can now become producers and owners of data, provided they are connected to some recording apparatus. In this context, the process of valorization does not come from replacing the body with the spirit, as in the rhetoric of creativity, but through the capitalization and appreciation of the most ubiquitous feature of the human that is shifting from the production of goods to the production of value.

The internal purpose (need) instructs an external purpose, thus creating an automaton. Without this projection, the automaton has no *raison d'être*, and it is upon this principle that the superiority of the human over technology is founded. Technology exists to fulfill human needs, not the other way around. The origin of human servitude is not to be found in the submission to a Golem, but in the subalternity of human beings who depend for their livelihood on the *placet* of systems that they themselves have nurtured. In other words, we are victims to an ignorance for which we alone are responsible. To understand this is to open ourselves to a kingdom of heaven—the human heritage, which is more diverse, liberal, and less tediously moralistic than what came before. Moral value and economic value are but two sides of the same coin, the same currency. The key lies in the currency, this trace that underlies value. **The process of economic valorization is also a process of cultural growth or education.**

The soul became the human soul not when it reached a certain brain mass, but when, through a series of fortuitous circumstances that we can retrospectively read as humanity's manifest destiny, it acquired technical supplements allowing it to overcome its shortcomings. The essence of the human as "the not yet determined animal" must therefore be sought in these technical supplements rather than organic foundations.[10] The latter make us equal to any other animal, while the supplement (what we are not and do not have) makes us what we are and points us towards what we must become. In this sense, the metaphysical meaning of original sin is simple: **Humans are the undetermined animal, intrinsically in need of progress.** To ignore this task that humanity has pursued thus far is to avoid engaging in a philosophy of history that strives for improvement, namely the very idea that Kant accurately referred to as "the education of the will," the only remedy for the endless will to power.

Of course, nothing perfectly straight can be made from the crooked timber of humanity, but humans are the only animals that can be educated. If I teach a horse to perform circus tricks, I turn it into a clown; if I teach a child to read and write, I make it more human. The problem, today as always, is that we are not educated enough, bound by the constraints of past habits, outdated perspectives, and even conceptual errors and superstitions. Consequently, the imperative for the new world that lies ahead—while not necessarily a utopia (a somewhat boring place, after all)—is undeniably the pursuit of a better and more equitable society than the one we leave behind. This requires shifting our focus from concerns over automation to concerns about education.

Addressing the pressing social and environmental issues at hand does not call for less progress, globalization, or capital, but rather demands the opposite: greater progress precisely because it would be pursued with awareness; a globalization that addresses the fears of a humanity feeling marginalized amidst an ever-changing world; and a new form of capital that empowers us to tackle challenges presented by an omnipotent nature. In this broader context, to recognize that in some ways we are subservient to nature like any other organism but masters of technology unlike other living beings or mechanisms is to restore political agency and, consequently, a sense of responsibility towards humans. It is not about depressing development but harnessing its

---

10   Cf. Arnold Gehlen, 1957, *Man in the Age of Technology* (New York: Columbia University Press, 1980). Plessner, Darwin, and Gehlen all agree that we are more able because we are weaker.

potential for the collective improvement of humanity, leading to what is effectively a happy growth.

The term *finis hominis* does not mean the *end* of humankind as catastrophists suggest, but the *end-goal* of humans—the pursuit of happiness. More than just happiness, it is a question of justice. And without a philosophy of history there can be no real justice because justice is teleological, it is done with something in mind, and this something can only be an organism. Justice does not apply to mechanisms or to something that is not alive. We honor the dead for the life they once hosted, and we think about future generations because they will inherit the world we shape. But to recognize the richness that lies in our finitude is to understand that, unlike machines, **we pursue ends precisely because we end.**

6. From Welfare to Webfare

Who foots the bill? In other words, **who can take charge of this virtuous process?** Keynes' vision of welfare required choices such as prioritizing between social security and healthcare. While the former was rightly favored, it came at the expense of the latter. Webfare, however, sets off from a completely different premise: rather than drawing resources from existing value, which is often inadequate like a blanket that is either too short or too narrow, we tap into an entirely new capital. This is where the real challenge lies and, in the years to come, our social, economic, and philosophical imagination will have to focus on this pursuit. Such a pursuit would involve mobilizing the intelligence of researchers and universities alongside various intermediate bodies to develop capitalization criteria. Having stressed the importance of theory so far, I will dedicate this final chapter to the exposition of a practical proposal that is already being implemented.[1]

6.1 Virtue Banks

The proposal is based on the European legislation on data portability, initially designed to protect privacy but applicable to numerous areas where capitalization goes hand in hand with protection. **Nowhere does it say that this value can only be exploited, as it currently is, only by**

---

1   As part of the research conducted at Scienza Nuova, The Institute for Advanced Studies in Torino, https://www.scienzanuovainstitute.com/

U.S. American liberalist platforms (who privatize profits) or Chinese communist platforms (who socialize profits but stifle the freedom of citizens through the control of nationalized platforms). Regulation 679/2016 grants users the right to request data from platforms.[2] Furthermore, as of March 25, 2022, users have the possibility to access syntactic data, which, as we have seen, generates genuine capitalization. Data portability includes syntactic data from social networks, shopping records, medical information, education, and much more.

At this point, an intermediary (banks, hospitals, universities, cooperatives, and so on) steps in, which I refer to as a "Virtue Bank" because they manage data for philanthropic purposes. These 'banks' seek permission from their clients to request their data from platforms and create a data bank. They act as "data intermediaries" (as per EU language), to which users grant the right to transfer their data and merge it with others to create new capital. After account holders have given authorization, the intermediaries can request data on their behalf, collect, interpret, and capitalize on it, aiming to monetize the newly formed capital. In this sense, the "virtue" in such Virtue Banks does not simply mean generic philanthropy. It means that they follow rational rules like those regulating pension funds that ensure that profit-seeking does not jeopardize the interest of clients and include remuneration for those who manage the process. Contributors who simply provide access to their data, willingly forego individual capitalization, which would be relatively modest in any case. Of course, one can also envision an alternative and more individual approach, such as parents accessing their small data reserves to fund their children's education once they are of age. However, why limit

---

2   General Data Protection Regulation (GDPR), Regulation (EU) 2016/679, *Official Journal of the European Union*, May 4, 2016, Section 2, Article 20 (1)"Right to Data Portability:" "The data subject shall have the right to receive the personal data concerning him or her, which he or she has provided to a controller, in a structured, commonly used and machine-readable format and have the right to transmit those data to another controller without hindrance from the controller to which the personal data have been provided." https://gdpr-info .eu/

this possibility to a select few when it can become a shared heritage of all humanity?

The Webfare proposed by the Virtue Banks consists of three inter-connected parts:

1) **a system of transparent privacy protection, where the Virtue Banks act as intermediaries managing authorizations for data use by commercial platforms.** What was once a free and often unconscious transfer of data is now conscious and monetizable, as platforms are required to pay the bank for these authorizations. In turn, the bank reserves the right to capitalize on the proceeds of such transfers and return the profits not directly to the account holders (the sums are too modest when distributed individually) but in the form of services, support, and education for socially vulnerable individuals.

2) **the development of a data interpretation system that would allow any institution motivated by clear philanthropic intentions to acquire data processing capabilities** (currently, these are largely centralized in U.S. American commercial platforms and Chinese state platforms). This fosters a virtuous circle of collaboration between academic research, industrial realities, and civil society, an untapped and underutilized potential at present.

3) **a capitalization system through the creation of an alternative platform with social purposes.** Once trust is established with the bank (with whom they already have a financial relationship), account holders, and hopefully an increasing number of third parties with social sustainability objectives, can access this alternative platform to voluntarily contribute valuable information for civic and philanthropic purposes.

6.2 Privacy Protection

Self-awareness, or understanding the origin of data, is the first step. Understanding that data is not just about privacy but is a wellspring of value sets the stage for this transformative endeavor. Public institutions, hand in hand with the Virtue Banks, have the fundamental task to raise this awareness. This mission is as vital as seeking justice, bolstering public education, and establishing an efficient national health care system. Once this awakening takes place, a multitude of options awaits: first, monetization, where individuals assert their right to capitalize on their data, forging an individualistic solution to the conundrum of value; second, finalization, or claiming the right to determine the purposes for which our data can be used; and finally, mutualization, championing the social redistribution of data value not for mere private gains but to the benefit of disadvantaged groups—a path that, in its very essence, aligns with the spirit of Webfare.

By employing explainable AI algorithms and practicing responsible data collection, we will promote digital literacy within the social community, increasing "big data literacy"—the awareness, comprehension, and critical reflection of citizens regarding big data practices, risks, and implications, and their ability to implement this newfound knowledge for a more conscious utilization of their interests.[3] **Within this framework, the first step is to recognize that the value of data is equally dependent on the mobilization of humanity and on how this mobilization is intercepted and interpreted by platforms.** Everything discussed thus far provides sufficient grounds for establishing the right to data acquisition, its foundation resting not on claims of ownership, but on the labor of mobilization performed by humans on platforms. Data, in essence, would not even exist were it not for platforms that host and maintain it, raising doubts about the legitimacy of requesting unfettered data ownership just in order to sell it. However, since platforms do not own mobilization (and the needs that drive it) nor the data it begets, it is precisely through the appeal to the latter that we can justify sharing for the purposes of an alternative capitalization.

The second step is negotiation through the quantification of the value of data. The digital data economy, with data freely accessible

---

3   Ina Sander, "Critical Big Data Literacy Tools: Engaging Citizens and Promoting Empowered Internet Usage," *Data & Policy* 2 (2020), June 11, 2020, doi:10.1017/dap.2020.5

through social media, free apps, and Internet access, reached €94 billion in Europe in 2019, with no signs of slowing down. This staggering figure does not even include personal user information in the form of Structured Query Language (SQL) data such as financial information whose access is limited by data protection laws. By combining the structured data at their disposal with unstructured data from commercial platforms, data cooperatives will generate a much larger market value. Additionally, acting as data trustees for people and their decisions on data access and usage, **Virtue Banks will negotiate data access terms with partners from industry, leading to significant economic profit.** In this context, we must forge innovative ways to quantify the data we generate through our interactions with platforms. Within this framework, ways need to be developed to quantify the data we produce in our relationship with platforms.

Efforts are already underway[4] to demand control over one's data[5] and quantify it.[6] A fortunate stroke of serendipity lies in European privacy protection laws, founded on the civil law principle of the inalienability of individual rights that can become the means to recognize the magnitude of data produced. In the realm of data quantification, a new law can be formulated: the less privacy, the greater the amount of data collected by platforms, and vice versa. **However, *quantifying data* is not yet *quantifying the value of data***, and therein lies the great challenge. Contrary to interpretations that see the digital economy as favoring the market over the company,[7] here the company supplants the market and renders the

---

4   Vili Lehdonvirta, Brendt Mittelstadt, et al., *Data Financing for Global Good: A Feasibility Study* (Oxford Internet Institute: University of Oxford, 2016).

5   Jean Tirole, *Economics for the Common Good* (Princeton, NJ: Princeton University Press, 2017).

6   Luca Bolognini and Isabella de Michelis di Slonghello, "An Introduction to The Right to Monetize (RTM)," *Diritto, Economia e Tecnologie della Privacy* (2018); Rodrigo Montes, Wilfried Sand-Zantman, and Tommaso Valletti, "The Value of Personal Information in Online Markets with Endogenous Privacy," *Management Science* 65: 3 (March 2019): 1342–1362.

7   Viktor Mayer-Schönberger and Thomas Ramge, *Reinventing Capitalism in the Age of Big Data* (London: Basic Books, 2018).

determination of public value impossible. Just what is the value of information that makes it possible to fly planes at full capacity based on passenger behavior data? This is a question that will never be answered if data acquisition remains the result of private negotiations between platforms and companies. If there were a market (and there will be one when data investors distinct from platforms enter the scene), there would be supply and demand and they will dictate the value. **The key to establishing a data market, and hence determining the value of data, lies in formulating public criteria for their interpretation.**

6.3 Interpretation

Commercial platforms interpret data on the basis of algorithms, whereas Virtue Banks can couple structured data with unstructured data (sourced from their members via commercial platforms), resulting in a much greater body of knowledge. This allows us to address a legitimate concern, namely, that harnessing the potential of big data demands the application of cutting-edge technologies and expertise. Public administrations, local health authorities, cooperative banks, universities, and museums, that is, the institutions that can be transformed into **Virtue Banks**, are smaller and less well-equipped hermeneutically than commercial platforms and are thus destined to succumb in the competition. Fortunately, Virtue Banks have a distinct advantage over their gargantuan commercial counterparts: they have structured data at disposal (bank account holders, members of a cooperative), and do not have to rely on algorithms to compute the social data of their members. This significantly reduces the inherent randomness of abductive reasoning. The application of cutting-edge technologies and fostering innovation become a paramount pursuit, and the path forward lies in leveraging **the intellectual capital** of researchers and universities that will support the Virtue Banks in devising hermeneutic criteria, which neither Silicon Valley nor Shanghai can monopolize.

Such an endeavor aligns with the theory of **a fourfold notion of truth**, which I explored in detail elsewhere.[8] This theory centers on the following premise: **Data, forming the ontological level, serves as *truth-bearer* in the sense that it does not inherently possess truth or meaning but plays a pivotal role by existing as a document that provides the raw material for interpretation.** Effective hermeneutics first demands the acknowledgment of the material basis of data, of its literal foundation as that which constitutes the object of recording, i.e., what I call the bearer of truth. This material basis consists in the enormous variety of human life forms that, when meticulously documented and collected, constitute a new ontological realm of data. All data, just like sensations, are real. However, being real is not the same as being true. This is why refining data is more complex than refining petroleum, though it requires significantly less investment and equipment and often just intelligence and intuition.

The technological level consists of *truth-makers*, that is, of the technical procedures employed to extract meaning and correlations from data. It is at this level that platforms with structured databases play a decisive role. They can secure a competitive advantage over large commercial platforms, provided that they can effectively compare their structured data with the colossal sea of big data offered by commercial behemoths. **This involves the cross-referencing of the semantic data already at disposal of institutions with the semantic and syntactic data produced by their members and obtained through data portability laws.** We find at this intersection the potentially greatest cognitive enterprise humanity can embark on. It is within reach of numerous actors, unlike the oligopoly of the current big players. Valuable correlations between lifestyles, diseases, educational trajectories, and financial prospects can be obtained through the combination of structured semantic data (e.g., preexisting conditions, career choices, mortgage agreements) and big data, both in its semantic (social media posts) and syntactic form (e.g., behavioral patterns of data producers).

---

8   Ferraris, *Doc-Humanity*, cit.

The rules of correlation forming the core of so-called 'data science' are a mixture of hermeneutic and epistemological precepts. Here are some examples: follow explicit, verifiable, and repeatable processes; remain cognizant of the context of data production; deconstruct problems analytically for data-driven solutions; remember that entities which are alike in known aspects may also be alike in unknown aspects; do not generalize conclusions drawn from limited or overanalyzed data sets; and try not to draw conclusions influenced by factors external to the data being examined.[9] The process must start with the premise that, contrary to popular belief, understanding reality does not diminish freedom; rather, the better we comprehend the reality in which we make our choices, the more freedom we have to make informed decisions, as our choices would be conditioned to a lesser extent by our limited understanding.

At the epistemological level of *truth-tellers*, it becomes imperative to move beyond the realm of mere interpretation and aim for explanations. Allow me to elaborate. Hermeneutics, the art of making connections and establishing correlations, is the task of technicians—be they hermeneuticians, semioticians, data scientists, or whatever nomenclature suits. These are individuals whose distinct prowess lies in processing data and deriving meaning from it not unlike the codebreakers of the German Enigma cipher, led by the ingenious Alan Turing at Bletchley Park, who were the early pioneers of computer science.

However, **it behooves us to recognize that the ability to interpret a code does not bestow universal scientific wisdom, as some semioticians and hermeneuticians of the last century might have misleadingly suggested (or perhaps, as we wished to believe in order to console ourselves).** Much like knowing the letters of the alphabet does not amount to possessing absolute knowledge, the outcome of deciphering Enigma would not have secured victory for the Allies without the strategic insight of experienced generals. This may seem obvious, but it is not. For instance, Google's ambitious proposition of extending a national healthcare service to the United States holds promise and virtue, given

---

9   Foster Provost and Tom Fawcett, "Data Science and its Relationship to Big Data and Data-Driven Decision Making," *Big Data* 1 (2013): 51–59.

the lack of universal healthcare in the country. Nevertheless, we must question the prudence of entrusting the medical care of uninsured American citizens to hermeneuticians, semioticians, or data scientists instead of skilled medical professionals. In other words, **the possession of standards and methods of interpretation must systematically coincide with appropriate scientific expertise in the relevant domain of analysis, whether economics, medicine, history, law, or any other domain of knowledge.**

However, none of this would make sense without the ultimate recipients of interpretation, the *truth-users*, namely humans, who stand at the beginning and end of this process. Recording, as a mechanical function, generates the system; consumption, as an organic function, produces value. Going back to what was said about human forms of life, this value production entails both primary production (where humans define what is good) and secondary production (where humans, through their mobilization, help automate production). This is why consumption, often considered labor's lesser sibling, emerges as a higher-order production—the vanguard of values—for it has always been the producer of use-value (without consumers, there would be no value in general). But, with the advent of widespread Web-based recording, consumption has now become the producer of exchange value.

6.4 Redistribution

Moving on, we come to the redistribution of data. **The current emerging post-industrialization landscape reveals a paradox: while automation guarantees greater availability of goods, it also leads to a rarefication of traditional job opportunities. This imbalance poses a threat to the system, for if consumers are unemployed because of automation, they cannot afford to purchase goods. To prevent a collapse, we must ensure that consumption produces new value.** This, in fact, is the most efficient and powerful self-sustaining form of capital in history that has yet to be leveraged. **As for commercial platforms, the absence of a data stock market renders it difficult to implement fair compensation**

policies aimed at redistributing the surplus value. Consider the taxation proposals set forth by China and already partly embraced by the United States and the European Union.[10] While some may fear that such redistribution endeavors might risk passing costs onto users, we must remember that platforms would lose all appeal if they ceased to provide services for free. The main impediment lies in the fact that, without a **data stock market,** it is very difficult to determine the value of data and apply appropriate tax pressure on these platforms.

Compensation, however, is not limited to the redistribution of tax revenue. It can also involve the expansion of areas offering free goods and services (thus leveraging the idea of "human heritage" in line with the commercial interests of platforms. Such an alignment is consistent with our overarching approach, where user contribution involves mobilization and platform contribution comprises recording and production. Gratuity should thus not be seen as a *common good* but as a ***collaborative product.*** This terminological differentiation is crucial, as it emphasizes that users do not claim a right to the capital obtained from data *capitalization* by platforms—such claims fall under the purview of state taxation. Instead, gratuity stands as a testament to their mobilization in the *production* of data. In this context, **Virtue Banks must engage in the sharing not of data itself but of its value.** If compensation involves an intervention on already capitalized data, then we are dealing with two fundamentally different processes.

First, there is the production of value through an alternative and autonomous capitalization, one distinct from that carried out by commercial platforms whose contribution is limited to the sharing of data with the Virtue Banks. Second, to avoid that the term "Virtue Bank" appear abusive or overly rhetorical, it is essential for the concept to embody genuine and transparent virtue. In other words, **the purpose of the Virtue Bank is not to reward account holders**—traditional banking and stock exchange services cater to those with financial assets. **Instead, it seeks to**

---

10   Naoki Matsuda, "Is China Considering a Data Tax on Big Tech? Signs Point to Yes," *Nikkei Asia*, November 22, 2021, https://asia.nikkei.com/Economy/Is-China-considering-a-data-tax-on-big-tech-Signs-point-to-yes

integrate the vast majority of humanity who may lack funds but possess valuable data into the economic playfield. This integration is achieved by opening an account in the bank, based first on data and then on liquid assets, offering a pathway for substantive, rather than merely formal, citizenship. From the perspective of Virtue Banks, the proceeds from data interpretation will be redistributed to users according to their economic needs or, alternatively, reinvested in projects aimed at promoting the well-being of the local community (e.g., the integration of vulnerable individuals, assistance for local research), following the mutualistic nature of data cooperatives.

The rationale behind this allocation diverges significantly from the conventional concepts of universal or citizenship incomes, which have been proposed over the past two centuries and gained momentum in recent decades, especially in response to the challenges posed by automation and its impact on employment. Instead, it rests on the idea of mutualization. "Mutualization" typically refers to the distribution of debt among many parties; in this case, however, we are dealing with a mutuality based not on debt but on credit. All parties involved in the process of capitalization generate value. However, those fortunate enough to possess existing sources of income willingly forgo personal profits in favor of a more substantial and meaningful redistribution. This is not a mere blanket redistribution to those without income, but rather a targeted and thoughtful approach based on data contributions.

Is such an initiative possible? From our perspective, yes. Current account holders who authorize the bank to retrieve and capitalize their *social* data already find themselves in a position of financial stability—they have bank accounts. It is also presumed that they are generous individuals, as they typically disapprove of the greed of *conquistadors* and commercial entities that hoard profits rightfully belonging to all of humanity. It would therefore seem rather odd if they claimed for themselves the profits generated by the capitalization of their data. After all, the fascinating aspect of data is that it becomes more valuable the more humans provide it. Therefore, it is reasonable to assume that many, if not the majority of these forward-thinking individuals, would warmly embrace an alternative scenario. For example, they might prefer to see the one billion dollars resulting from capitalization not merely distributed among one million account holders (resulting in meager one thousand dollars per year, or less than one hundred dollars per month), but rather channeled towards granting ten thousand dollars to one hundred thousand people in need. These individuals may not currently have a traditional bank account but possess a cellphone and have opened a data account with the Virtue Bank, thus increasing the data capital that sets them on the path towards substantial citizenship. For rights and documents hold limited worth without the added dimension of financial assets. Conversely, the voluntary relinquishment of one's share of capitalization is neither forced nor illiberal, as those who have embraced the alternative capitalization process have done so willingly, with the freedom to choose either to abstain from participating or to capitalize their data in a privatized form.

Epilogue: From Being to Being-Together

One last consideration. I imagine many readers may wonder whether the transition from production to consumption represents yet another blow to humanity, akin to the historical humiliations inflicted by Copernicus (we are not at the center of the universe), Darwin (we are animals like any other), and Freud (consciousness is a byproduct of irrational impulses). As pure consumers, seemingly incapable of crafting even a simple pin, might we unwittingly subject ourselves to a moral and cognitive decline, ushering in an era of ineptitude and ignorance? I am acutely aware of this potential risk and this is the reason why I insist on the importance of investing the newfound resources of humanity primarily in education.

Education has the power of bestowing upon humanity the spiritual resources needed to unlock its full potential and replace idleness with the joys and responsibilities of human coexistence. For, let us not forget, **being for *homo faber* is only incidentally a being-together.** We may gather in groups to work, but as we witnessed during times of technological advancements and lockdowns, this togetherness can be severed without affecting productivity. As we know, this elicited controversial reactions, but it was typically regarded as a downside rather than a positive aspect. While remote work has certainly offered respite from forced proximity and workplace conflicts, the human being as a social animal craves physical closeness and spiritual affinity—elements that can exist independently of the proximity of bodies. In other words, the coexistence of *homo faber* is accidental, whereas the coexistence of *homo sapiens* is essential and far from having been systematically realized throughout history. In the majority of cases, it has been an exception rather than the norm. I am thinking of ritual situations, ceremonies (traditions, celebrations, pop concerts), or elite phenomena such as court life or salons. All these cases should not be disregarded, for they demonstrate how humanity can come together in communities driven not by material needs but by demands for representation and symbolic consumption, emphasizing the social aspect of coexistence.

I can spend ten days in Bayreuth listening to Wagner's complete works and feel like I am simply fulfilling a social obligation and responsibility. Similarly, each of us, some with conviction and others out of conformism, may participate in a demonstration for gender freedom or environmental sustainability. Yet, it is precisely a different type of humanity—long living and freed from the obligations and conflicts that often arise from *homo faber's* interactions—that can develop its most significant attribute: reciprocal care. Rooted in our animal past, it manifests as tenderness, kindness, and understanding—the quintessence of being human, or an *homo homini deus*, which is nothing more than a *homo homini lupus* transformed through culture and education. This is not about jumping, marching, parading, or worshipping (all perfectly human activities, of course), but about engaging in a relationship not with multitudes but with the individuals next to us. We might discover them as friends, foes, or even just as someone indifferent, but through our shared culture and history, they can, though not necessarily, become objects of our interlocution or our care.

I am well aware that I venture into utopian territory, and by far. However, on one hand, if we recognize that being human is not merely a fixed state but an ongoing process that began millions of years ago and continues indefinitely, it appears that the best bet lies in promoting the indefinite progress of our species. On the other hand, if we focus solely on the disadvantages and potential threats looming in the future, not only will we deny ourselves the sweetness of hope, but we may also inadvertently enact a self-fulfilling prophecy that turns our nocturnal terrors into daytime reality.

Bibliography

Abrandi, Laura, Carlo Cambini, and Laura Rondi, "Artificial Intelligence, Firms and Consumer Behavior: A Survey," *Journal of Economic Surveys* 36 (2022): 969–991.

Anderson, Chris, "The End of Theory: The Data Deluge Makes the Scientific Method Obsolete," *Wired*, June 23, 2008, https://www.wired.com/2008/06/pb-theory/

Andrejevic, Mark, "Big Data, Big Questions: The Big Data Divide," *International Journal of Communication* 8 (2014): 1673–1689.

Bolognini, Luca and Isabella de Michelis di Slonghello, "An Introduction to The Right to Monetize (RTM)," *Diritto, Economia e Tecnologie della Privacy* (2018).

Carpo, Mario, *Beyond Digital: Design and Automation at the End of Modernity* (Cambridge, MA: The MIT Press, 2023).

Carpo, Mario, *The Second Digital Turn: Design Beyond Intelligence* (Cambridge, MA: The MIT Press, 2017)

Dagnes, Joselle and Angelo Salento, eds., *Prima i fondamentali. L'economia della vita quotidiana tra profitto e benessere* (Milano: Feltrinelli, 2022).

Deleuze, Gilles and Félix Guattari, *Anti-Oedipus: Capitalism and Schizophrenia* (New York: Viking Press, 1972).

Derrida, Jacques, *Of Grammatology* (Baltimore and London: The Johns Hopkins University Press, 1976).

Favaretto, Maddalena, Eva De Clercq, and Bernice Simone Elger, "Big Data and Discrimination: Perils, Promises and Solutions. A Systematic Review," *Journal of Big Data* 6: 12 (2019), https://doi.org/10.1186/s40537-019-0177-4

Ferraris, Maurizio, *Agostino: Fare la verità* (Bologna: il Mulino, 2022).

Ferraris, Maurizio, *Doc-Humanity* (Tübingen: Mohr Siebeck, 2022).

Ferraris, Maurizio, *Documentality: Why It Is Necessary to Leave Traces* (New York: SUNY Press, 2012).

Ferraris, Maurizio, *Hysteresis: The External World* (Edinburgh: Edinburgh University Press, forthcoming in 2024).

Ferraris, Maurizio, *Manifesto of New Realism* (New York: SUNY Press, 2014).

Ferraris, Maurizio and Guido Saracco, *Tecnosofia: Tecnologia e umanesimo per una scienza nuova* (Rome and Bari: Laterza, 2023).

Floridi, Luciano, *Il verde e il blu: Idee ingenue per migliorare la politica* (Milano: Cortina, 2022).

Floridi, Luciano, *Philosophy and Computing: An Introduction* (London and New York: Routledge, 1999).

Floridi, Luciano, *The 4th Revolution: How the Infosphere is Reshaping Human Reality* (Oxford: Oxford University Press, 2014).

Floridi, Luciano, *The Logic of Information: A Theory for Philosophy as Conceptual Design* (Oxford: Oxford University Press, 2019).

Foster, John, *The Case for Idealism* (London: Routledge, 1982).

Frey, Carl Benedikt and Michael A. Osborne, "The Future of Employment: How Susceptible Are Jobs to Computerisation?," Working paper published by the Oxford Martin Programme on the Impact of Future Technology, September 1, 2013, https://www.oxfordmartin.ox.ac.uk/publications/the-future-of-employment/

Garicano, Luis and Esteban Rossi-Hansberg, "Organization and Inequality in a Knowledge Economy," *The Quarterly Journal of Economics*, 121:4 (2016): 1383–1435.

Gehlen, Arnold, *Man in the Age of Technology* (New York: Columbia University Press, 1980).

Graeber, David, *Bullshit Jobs. A Theory* (New York: Simon & Schuster, 2018).

Helbing, Dirk, *Next Civilization: Digital Democracy and Socio-Ecological Finance—How to Avoid Dystopia and Upgrade Society by Digital Means* (Cham: Springer, 2021).

Heller, Ágnes, *Towards a Marxist Theory of Value* (Carbondale, IL: Southern Illinois University, 1972).

Keynes, John M., *The General Theory of Employment, Interest and Money* (London: Macmillan, 1936).

Lehdonvirta, Vili, Brendt Mittelstadt, et al., *Data Financing for Global Good: A Feasibility Study* (Oxford Internet Institute: University of Oxford, 2016).

Lévy, Pierre, *Collective Intelligence: Mankind's Emerging World in Cyberspace* (New York: Plenum Trade, 1997).

Lyotard, Jean-François, "Les immatériaux," *Art & Text*, 1985.

Lyotard, Jean-François, *Libidinal Economy* (Bloomington, IN: Indiana University Press, 1974).

Markets and Markets, "Emotion Detection and Recognition (EDR) Market," 2022, https://www.marketsandmarkets.com/pdfdownloadNew.asp?id=23376176

Marx, Karl, *Critique of the Gotha Programme*, in Marx and Engels, *Selected Works*, Vol. 3 (Moscow: Progress Publishers, 1970, pp.13-30).

Marx, Leo, *The Machine in the Garden: Technology and the Pastoral Ideal in America* (New York: Oxford University Press, 1964).

Matsuda, Naoki, "Is China Considering a Data Tax on Big Tech? Signs Point to Yes," *Nikkei Asia*, November 22, 2021, https://asia.nikkei.com/Economy/Is-China-considering-a-data-tax-on-big-tech-Signs-point-to-yes

Mayer-Schönberger, Viktor and Thomas Ramge, *Reinventing Capitalism in the Age of Big Data* (New York: Basic Books, 2018).

Meadows, Donella H., Dennis L. Meadows, Jørgen Randers, and William W. Behrens III, *The Limits to Growth* (New York: Universe Books, 1972).

Meijer, Ellen, "Blockchain and Our Planet: Why Such High Energy Use?", *Pre-Sustainability*, June 6, 2022, https://pre-sustainability.com/articles/blockchain-and-our-planet-why-such-high-energy-use/

Montes, Rodrigo, Wilfried Sand-Zantman, and Tommaso Valletti, "The Value of Personal Information in Online Markets with Endogenous Privacy," *Management Science* 65: 3 (March 2019): 1342–1362.

Nussbaum, Martha C., *The Fragility of Goodness: Luck and Ethics in Greek Tragedy and Philosophy* (Cambridge and New York: Cambridge University Press, 1986).

OECD, "Data on the Future of Work," https://www.oecd.org/future-of-work/reports-and-data/data-infographics.htm, last accessed July 26, 2023.

Paglieri, Fabio, *La disinformazione felice: Cosa ci insegnano le bufale* (Bologna: il Mulino, 2020).

Palmer, Michael, "Data is the New Oil," *ANA Marketing Maestros*, November 3, 2006, https://ana.blogs.com/maestros/2006/11/data_is_the_new.html

Phillips, Leigh and Michal Rozworski, *The People's Republic of Walmart: How the World's Biggest Corporations are Laying the Foundation for Socialism* (London: Verso, 2019).

Piketty, Thomas, *Capital in the Twenty-first Century* (Cambridge, MA: Harvard University Press, 2013).

Provost, Foster and Tom Fawcett, "Data Science and its Relationship to Big Data and Data-Driven Decision Making," *Big Data* 1 (2013): 51–59.

Sandel, Michael, *The Tyranny of Merit: What's Become of the Common Good?* (New York: Farrar, Straus and Giroux, 2020).

Sander, Ina, "Critical Big Data Literacy Tools: Engaging Citizens and Promoting Empowered Internet Usage," *Data & Policy* 2 (2020), June 11, 2020, doi:10.1017/dap.2020.5

Searle, John R., "What Your Computer Can't Know," *The New York Review*, October 9, 2014.

Searle, John R., *Making the Social World: The Structure of Human Civilization* (Oxford and New York: Oxford University Press, 2010).

Searle, John R., *The Construction of Social Reality* (New York: Free Press, 1995).

Sonderegger, Paul, "Data Hits Peak Metaphor," March 4, 2021, https://paulsonderegger.com/2021/03/04/data-hits-peak-metaphor/

Sonderegger, Paul, "Three Things You Should Know About the Hidden Data Economy," *Paul Sonderegger* (blog), November 23, 2020, https://paulsonderegger.com/2020/11/23/three-things-you-should-know-about-the-hidden-data-economy/

Susskind, Daniel, *A World Without Work: Technology, Automation, and How We Should Respond* (London: Allen Lane, 2020).

Suzman, James, *Work: A History of How We Spend Our Time* (London: Bloomsbury, 2020).

Teilhard de Chardin, Pierre, *The Vision of the Past* (New York: Harper & Row, 1967).

Tirole, Jean, *Economics for the Common Good* (Princeton, NJ: Princeton University Press, 2017).

Toffler, Alvin, *The Third Wave* (New York: William Morrow, 1980.

West, Darrell M., "What Happens if Robots Take the Jobs? The Impact of Emerging Technologies on Employment and Public Policy," *Brookings*, October 26, 2015, https://www.brookings.edu/articles/what-happens-if-robots-take-the-jobs-the-impact-of-emerging-technologies-on-employment-and-public-policy/

Zuboff, Shoshana, *The Age of Surveillance Capitalism: The Fight for a Human Future at the New Frontier of Power* (London: Profile Books, 2019).

Printed in the USA
CPSIA information can be obtained
at www.ICGtesting.com
JSHW011445051024
71100JS00008B/49